Alaska Rainbows

Flyfishing For Trout, Salmon & Other Alaskan Species

Larry Tullis

Frank Amato Publications, Inc.
P.O. Box 82112, Portland, Oregon 97282
503•653•8108 • www.amatobooks.com

All photographs by Larry Tullis unless otherwise noted.
Book & Cover Design: Kathy Johnson

Printed in Singapore

Softbound ISBN: 1-57188-251-0   UPC: 0-66066-00440-6
Hardbound ISBN: 1-57188-274-X
3 5 7 9 10 8 6 4 2

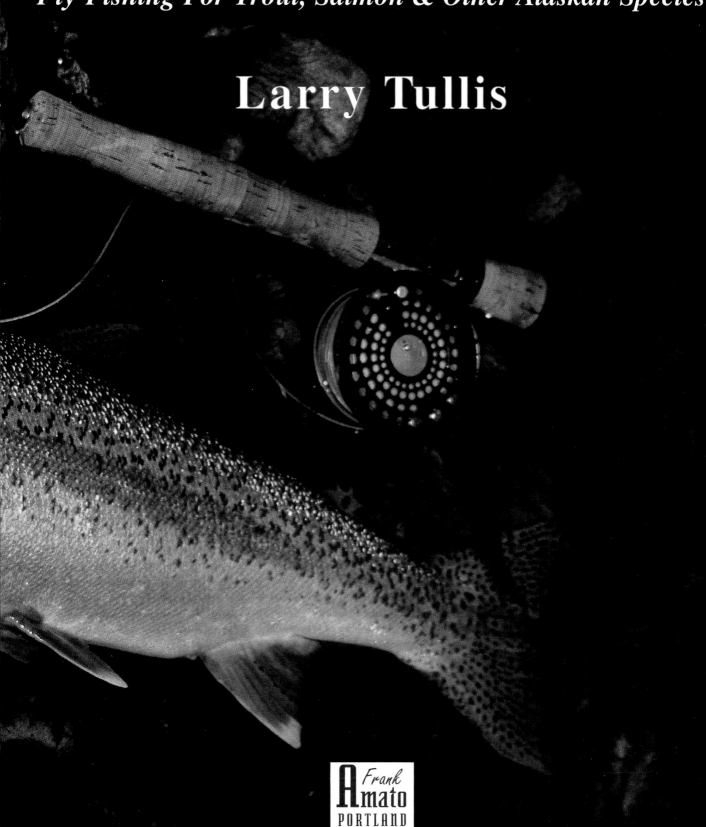

Alaska Rainbows

Fly-Fishing For Trout, Salmon & Other Alaskan Species

Larry Tullis

Frank
Amato
PORTLAND

FISHING SEASONS CHART

	March	April	May	June	July	August	September	October	November
Rainbow Trout	Spawn, Streamers	Spawn, Runoff	Dry Flies, Streamers, Nymphs, Eggs	Dry Flies, Nymphs, Eggs	Egg Season	Egg Flies, Flesh Flies & Streamers	Streamers, Flesh Flies & Egg Flies	Frozen Up	
Arctic Char Dolly Varden	Streamers	Runoff	Streamers	Streamers, Eggs	Streamers, Eggs, Spawn	Streamers, Eggs, Spawn	Streamers	Frozen Up	
Grayling	Spawn	Spawn, Runoff	Nymphs, Dries	Dries, Nymphs	Dry Flies, Nymphs & Egg Flies	Dry Flies, Nymphs & Egg Flies	Dry Flies & Nymphs	Frozen Up	
Lake Trout	Good At Iceoff, Streamers	Streamer-Fish Lakes	Streamers	Streamers	Streamers, Fish Deep in Lakes	Spawn Streamers In Shallows	Streamers	Frozen Up	
Northern Pike	Lakes Iceoff, Streamers	Streamers, Poppers in Lakes	Streamers, Poppers & Sliders	Streamers, Poppers & Sliders	Streamers	Streamers	Streamers	Frozen Up	
King Salmon	In Ocean	Fresh Runs	Fresh Runs	Spawn	Spawn	Dead or In Ocean	In Ocean	In Ocean	
Chum Salmon	In Ocean	In Ocean	In Ocean	Fresh Runs	Spawn	Dead or In Ocean	In Ocean	In Ocean	
Sockeye Salmon	In Ocean	In Ocean	Start Runs	Fresh Runs	Spawn	Spawn/Die	In Ocean	In Ocean	
Pink Salmon	In Ocean	In Ocean	In Ocean	Fresh Runs	Abundant	Spawn/Die	In Ocean	In Ocean	
Silver Salmon	In Ocean	In Ocean	In Ocean	Runs Begin	Abundant	Abundant	Spawn/Die	In Ocean	

FLY PATTERN GUIDE

	March	April	May	June	July	August	September	October	November
Dry Flies	Gnats	Gnats	Stoneflies, Caddis, mayflies, Gnats	Caddis, Mayflies, Gnats	Only in Landlocked Waters	Some Dry-Fly Action	Some Dry-Fly Action	None	
Nymphs	Fair	Good	Excellent	Good	Landlocked	Landlocked	Fair	Frozen Up	
Streamers	Excellent	Excellent	Excellent	Good	Good to Poor	Poor to Excellent	Excellent	Frozen Up	
Egg Patterns	Good	Good	Good	Good to Excellent	Excellent	Excellent	Good	Frozen Up	
Flesh Flies	Good	Good	Good	Fair	Poor	Excellent	Excellent	Frozen Up	
Fry/Smolt	Good	Excellent	Excellent	Fair	Poor	Poor	Poor	Frozen Up	
Salmon Patterns	All in Ocean	Kings	Kings	Chum Sockeye, King, Pink	Silver, Pink, Chum, king, Sockeye	Silver, Sockeye	Silvers	In Ocean	

Contents

I
Introduction

A FLASH OF SILVER AND A TWITCH OF THE indicator was more than enough to know a trout had taken the egg fly pattern. The strike was met with resistance that seemed to trigger an explosion. The water erupted several times as the huge rainbow threw itself into a series of wild leaps that ripped up the previously tranquil run. It screamed downstream at a speed that threatened to throw the fly feel apart and break the tippet just from sheer speed.

It was time to clamber to shore and sprint after the fish that already had all the fly line and 50 yards of backing out and still showed no signs of stopping. The fish finally stopped in the flat just above the next riffle and shook its head but it still took a couple minutes to reel up the slack as I walked the gravel bar to where the fish hovered. As soon as the line came tight again, the rainbow showed that it still had plenty of energy by making a blazing run upstream, against the current, but still getting into the backing again anyway. The gradually tiring fish ended its run in another

series of leaps that almost took it into the alder thicket on the far bank. This time my angle allowed me to lead it back to my shore as the line was reeled up once more.

It got close, but as often happens, this slab-sided trophy wasn't done yet and took off on another run across stream, jumping clear of the water in a classic pose and then swam downstream a few yards. That took its main reserves and it came in grudgingly but steadily. The fish slid up into shallow water and finally lay on its side, for the first time showing its full size. I lay the marked rod next to the fish, it was just shy of 30 inches long and had about a 20-inch girth, which made it well over 12 pounds.

I wanted to revive and release the fish quickly so I backed the hook out with my hemostats and held the lower jaw of the fish between my thumb and forefinger, allowing oxygenated water to wash over the fish's gills. It stirred but remained in place and the big female's body language said it was gaining its strength back fast. In one motion she

Author with a 29-incher.

turned away in a boil that gave me a shower and powered her back into the depths.

I was about to relax and absorb the experience but a movement out of the corner of my eye instantly put me on guard. A big brown bear erupted out of the tall grass 50 yards downstream and charged full-bore towards me. It only took me one second to realize that the 700-pound bear was chasing a salmon up the riffle, and not me, but it still put my heart up in my throat anyway and got me backing up and away. The bruin caught the salmon, saw me as I yelled the customary "Hey Bear" and lumbered off to eat its prize, hardly caring that I was even there.

That was a memorable experience for me and I have hundreds more from the time I've spent in Alaska. There is something about the wilderness experience that awakens primordial feelings in the civilized man and makes every second of life seem so much more vibrant and intense than it can in the city.

Wild Alaska rainbow trout get into your dreams in a way few things do. Maybe it's the fact that they can twist an 8-weight rod double and still take you well into your backing or maybe it's the wild and beautiful environs where

they are found. Whether you're after over-sized native rainbow trout and salmon or just want a wilderness escape, Alaska is one of the few places where this unique kind of adventure can still be experienced.

This book is dedicated to teaching the angler about Alaska rainbow trout, their habits, their foods, the fly patterns and techniques that work for them and a little about backcountry travel and the marvelous things you might experience while there. If you're looking for a book that exploits secret spots, this isn't your book. I'll mention specific trout waters only in passing or in a general list and concentrate mostly on the trout themselves, the modern flies and flyfishing methods that are effective and what fly-fishers need to know about travel in the Alaska wilderness. This information will allow you to research the lodges or put a do-it-yourself trip together and know what to expect when you get there.

Some of the waters have very fragile ecosystems and exploitation would hurt them. On the other hand, no one can keep a place secret for long. It's human nature to explore, and soon someone will find your secret spot. You can hope it will be someone who has a conservation ethic

Brown stonefly and the fly that caught the trout.

Fall on the Alaskan tundra.

Tundra blueberries.

and is adamant about protecting the fishery for the future. That is why I can't feel bad about sharing the things in this book with fly-fishers. Even remote waters need friends in today's world or enemies will likely exploit the resources to their max and then move on, leaving a wasteland.

I won't include too much on steelhead, even though native Alaska rainbows are very migratory, like steelhead, and are often known to go into salt water as they travel between rivers. Steelhead have very different habits and there are a variety of great books already dedicated to them. People disagree on how closely Alaska's steelhead and native rainbows are biologically related but most experienced anglers notice a distinct difference in their habits, the streams they prefer, the ways they feed, and the techniques that will work for each.

Alaska Rainbows will concentrate on the native trout and salmon found most often in the streams and lakes of the trophy trout areas in the Bristol Bay and Southwest Alaska rivers, but the information shared here will help your fishing anywhere you trout and salmon fish. Alaska's rainbow trout populations are highly dependent on the prolific runs of salmon for food and so there will be a discussion of Pacific salmon and how the trout relate to them. Salmon, char, lake trout, grayling and pike fishing strategies will be included as a chapter because anglers often fish for them and rainbow trout in the same waters or on the same trip.

We will also get into the different kinds of trips that are available to the angler in Alaska, preparations for each and lists of recommended equipment. By the end of the book you should understand Alaska and its sport fish like few people do and be excited to travel there someday soon yourself. If you have been there before, this will help you prepare for another adventure. Expensive lodges are the nicest and easiest way to fish Alaska but I don't believe Alaskan adventures should be limited only to the wealthy that can afford high-class lodges. I will include info on do-it-yourself trips that will save you thousands and I'll show

Tundra fly trap.

you how to plan an Alaskan adventure and deal with the animals you might see while there.

Far Eastern Russia has an emerging rainbow sport fishery that is similar in many ways to Alaska and will be discussed in one chapter. Now, let's go to Alaska.

Sunset on Upper Alagnak River trout stream.

II
Alaska Trout Habits & Foods

A Biographical History

THE POLAR ICE CAPS MELTED BACK FROM THEIR grip on North America thousands of years ago. Coastal region anadromous fish began exploring, spawning in and populating rivers further and further north, as they became habitable. Animals have the instinct to expand and fill suitable ecological niches that aren't already filled and the curious aquatic explorers that ended up in Alaska adapted to the conditions there and became new residents of this prime real estate.

Anadromous salmon used the rivers for spawning and then died. Trout also used the rivers for spawning and

Once covered in ice, now this glacial valley calls for adventure.

didn't die but discovered a source of food in salmon eggs, salmon flesh and salmon fry. Add to that, leeches, whitefish minnows, lamprey eels, insects, sculpins, mice, lemmings, and so on, and they found enough to feed on year-round. Some months were sparse but there was always the huge influx of food during the salmon runs that provided adequate food to perpetuate the species.

Soon trout and char populated most of the same waterways that salmon frequented and lost some of their anadromous tendencies, preferring to winter in the lakes instead of returning to the ocean. River systems with lakes and large populations of salmon became the best trophy trout waters as well. Some trout became separated from salmon areas and survived by limiting their size and populations, feeding on sparse insect hatches and minnows.

Alaskan rainbow trout have had to adapt to conditions that are quite different from those in most other areas of North America. The streams and lakes in Alaska are more sterile and often relatively devoid of the insect populations that support their southern cousins. Few trout in Alaska stay in the rivers where they are found during summer, throughout the year. Some are very migratory and individuals will often visit several rivers, lakes and the ocean during the course of a year, probably owing to their close ties to anadromous steelhead and salmon and their instinctual need to go where the food is.

Their foods are varied at times but it often comes all at once in huge volumes of one item. This has made the rainbows very adaptable and opportunistic. With the increased fishing pressure caused by today's sophisticated angler, trout also have had to adapt to the human presence. For a while in Alaska, trout were generally regarded as a

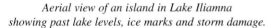

*Aerial view of an island in Lake Iliamna
showing past lake levels, ice marks and storm damage.*

second-class fish to the more commercially important salmon species. Trout were caught for sport and indiscriminately killed for people or dogs to eat and populations went down significantly in many waters. Although large and sometimes plentiful, they are much longer lived and slower growing than salmon so populations couldn't rebound quickly.

Luckily, there was a core of concerned anglers and wildlife managers that saw fit to protect the fragile trout and their environment. Trophy trout areas were named and the fish protected from overharvest. Today, these prime waters have fly-fishing-only or artificial-lure and fly-only regulations and reduce drastically or eliminate completely the harvest of Alaska rainbows. Most rainbow waters have gotten better in recent years and there is no sign of a reversal. The trout seem to keep getting bigger and more numerous despite increased angling pressure. A tribute to far-sighted management that doesn't rely on inferior hatchery fish but preserves the integrity of the natural bloodline through regulations and habitat protection.

Trout Habits

There are many things that induce trout to take flies and this section will cover these habits so you may better understand them. These traits are seen in many game fish so they should give you a better understanding of fish in general.

Are trout smart? No, not compared to us. Their brains are the size of a pea and they can't analyze or remember much input. What they do have is an incredible set of programmed survival instincts and extra-fast reactions to small amounts of information. A trout can react as much as 7 times faster than humans to stimuli such as taste, danger or aggression. A trout takes in small amounts of information and then reacts to it quickly so it seems trout are selective or quite educated when they reject our flies. They really have just narrowed down their choices to one or two aspects of their foods and if your flies don't reflect those items, they will be instantly rejected. The size, shape, action or color of your fly might be important but usually not everything at once. It's important to know all the reasons a trout will take a fly so you can adapt to constantly changing conditions that occur on all trout waters, so let's get into those things.

Basic hunger is one part of a trout's survival instinct. It is driven to eat more calories than the energy it expends to live and reproduce. If not, it will waste away and die. Their survival instinct won't let that happen so trout can adapt to any environment that has food enough for both its old and young. It's this innate need to feed that has produced some interesting side effects.

Curiosity is one way trout interact and learn from their environment. Without curiosity they would likely starve

Decaying king salmon provide nutrients for rainbow trout.

when faced with a depletion of their programmed foodstuffs. Trout are the masters of their environment and are constantly exploring and testing the limits of their world. They often sample drifting twigs, aquatic vegetation, minnows, terrestrial and aquatic insects and even small rodents. I've seen them eat carelessly tossed cigarette butts, strike indicators, cheese puffs, corn chips, white bread, bubble gum, hot dog pieces, chicken bones, split shot and other items that definitely are not part of their native environment.

This aspect of trout habits allows fly fishers an advantage because anglers are offering the trout many chances to sample new items (your flies). I'm convinced that many times trout and salmon take our flies mostly out of curiosity. That would explain why the hot fly patterns keep changing from week to week. The new flies are sampled and then found to be bad for their survival and are subsequently rejected. Because of this curiosity, trying new and different fly patterns often proves to be an advantage.

Aggression is associated with two different trout habits. One is **aggravation**. Aggravated fish lash out at the source of the disturbance. In fly-fishing, that aggravation is often a fly that is, time and time again, drifted or swung by a fish. Ever wonder why you can make 25 casts to the same water and then you get a hit on the 26th? It's often an aggravated fish trying to put an end to the repeated annoyance.

A related occurrence is what is termed an "**artificial hatch**". Here again, the fly is presented multiple times to the same fish and it suddenly starts feeding, as if the abundance of the item turned on a feeding switch.

The second type of aggression is the **territoriality** associated with spawning activity and prime feeding lies. When spawning, a trout will stake out its territory and usually the male will defend it from interlopers trying to steal his woman, spawning bed or his mate's eggs. He will chase away competitors and smaller fish who are looking to feed on eggs. If he gets close enough, he'll bite the interloper, which in your case may turn out to be your fly. He's not really feeding but the result is the same. The female also takes in flies without the intent to feed because she is a fastidious housekeeper and tries to remove foreign items that come into her nest area (i.e., your fly).

There is a philosophical opposition to fishing over spawning fish. Streams should be closed if catch-and-release fishing is found to be detrimental to the resource. Much of our fishing strategies, however, revolve around spawning-related activities such as fishing to prespawn steelhead, salmon and trout as they run up the rivers. My personal studies and observation shows that it doesn't seem to affect trout much, as long as you don't wade on their spawning beds and crush their eggs. They become very sigle-minded about spawning. Spawning trout that are caught-and-released quickly and properly go right back to what they were doing. On top of that, 50 to 90 percent of the fish caught in and around spawning areas are not actually spawning but are what I term "spawn groupies" or fish that are attracted by the spawning activity and the feeding opportunity it represents. Most trophy trout waters are closed to fishing during the rainbow spawn but trout exploit the salmon spawn as well, making them readily accessible to the summer angler.

The larger trout usually take up what's called a "prime feeding lie" and guard it from intruders, so not only do these trout feed here heavily but they also defend their territory. Both things can result in a hookup, using imitations of natural foods or imitations of interlopers (minnows, lampreys, etc.).

As food becomes more abundant, large trout will tolerate many more individuals in their feeding areas. The salmon spawn and the salmon fry migration are two times when big trout will group up heavily to feed.

The **baseball reaction** is like when someone throws you a baseball and says, "Think fast." Your natural reaction is to catch or dodge the ball. When a fly suddenly enters into a fish's personal space, the fish is put into a catch-it-or-dodge-it state of mind also. Chances are good that it will grab a streamer fly, egg, nymph or large attractor dry fly that suddenly enters its strike zone.

Another similar habit is the **intercept response.** It's what a trout does when it's not actively feeding but a food item comes right to the fish. Rather than dodge it or let it slide by, they bite the food and depending on the taste or their attitude will swallow or reject it. This state, when the fish isn't actively feeding or has seemingly selective behavior, is often associated with cold water (under 42 degrees F.), warm water (over 68 degrees), clear water with high sun intensity, an increase in fishing pressure, and weather or barometer changes.

It illustrates a very important part of trout fishing called the "strike zone." **Strike zones** are the areas that trout will move within to take a fly. In a normal strike zone, trout may move 3 to 24 inches to take a fly. Large strike zones can be 10 feet or more and small strike zones might be 1/2 to 3 inches. This should emphasize the need to get accurate drifts to trout that are not feeding aggressively.

The **fly drift level** is a very important aspect relating to strike zones. On days when the fish are charging your fly, relax and enjoy the action because the level at which your fly drifts is less important. When they seem to have lockjaw, realize that they will take your fly but you must concentrate on drifting it right at the nose of the fish (to get it into the smallest strike zone). When you do, you'll likely trigger an intercept response and catch fish when others get skunked (see the techniques section). The key is to adjust the strike indicator, line, weight and fly and presentation to fine-tune your drift.

Super-natural stimulus is what happens when fish are presented with a fly that is much bigger and gaudier than their natural food but which looks good to eat. It might be simple curiosity but also might be the same thing that makes us go to all-you-can-eat joints—if some is good, more is better. Over-sized egg patterns and large, gaudy attractor nymphs, streamers and dry flies are of particular interest to Alaska rainbows until they get selective from fishing pressure. Trout also respond to these extra-large flies when not feeding actively because they are opportunistic. Sometimes they just can't pass by a big meal.

The term "**opportunistic**" refers to trout that see an opportunity to feed and automatically do so as a matter of survival feeding or because of curiosity. They might not see many swimming mice in a week but mice often trigger an opportunistic response from the bigger fish.

Imprinting can also trigger an almost automatic feeding response. Trout get keyed in on eating certain foods when they are abundant or regularly available. Because of repeated feeding on a particular item, they get conditioned to that food and anytime that food comes into their strike zone, and matches the imprint on their mind, it is automatically taken because it is considered a "safe" food item. Size, shape, action and color are important here. For dry flies, the wing silhouette, surface impression or natural drift is important. Nymphs and streamers need the right shape, size and movement. Egg patterns for selective trout often need to be the right color, size and shape, plus drift naturally in a trout's often small strike zone.

Parallel imprint responses are closely related to imprinting. Imprints of food items gradually fade as a once-abundant food item becomes unavailable. I believe that the imprint is still there but gradually fades for 1 to 2 months, like an old faded photograph. Rainbows don't have an active memory like humans but do get conditioned to repeated stimuli. Just as we have memories triggered by a smell, taste, sound, name, something we see or a feeling, trout will often take flies that remind them of their fading imprint. Exact imitations of bygone foods seldom work at this time. Just as our memories are usually better or brighter than the original happening, white, bright or contrasting light/dark colors often trigger feeding. Think of these flies as cartoon versions of the real thing.

White-winged attractor dry flies, nymphs or streamers all do well at times, as do peacock herl bodies, brown or black hackle, white rubber-legs and flash. Think of an attractor fly as something that looks better than the original, or an abstract version, and you'll realize why trout are sometimes susceptible to attractor flies and why they trigger a now-faded imprint feeding response.

One of the few things that break a trout's selectivity on salmon eggs is attractor nymphs like the Flash Nymph or a dry fly like the Egg Dry Fly, something similar to what it was feeding on a month before. Attractor dry flies work best after the hatch it suggests is over. The hatch, nymph availability, or minnow-feeding activity may have been over for a few hours or up to a month or more but the imprint is still there and attractor flies will often trigger a response. Try them between hatches, when trout get extremely selective on eggs, or between times when a trout is actively feeding. Attractor flies are taken because of fading imprints, opportunism, curiosity and super-natural stimulus as well as regular feeding responses to hunger.

Trout habit categories are four basic groups of trout habits that relate to the abundance or lack of fishing pressure combined with the trout's frame of mind. Because of the migratory nature of Alaska's rainbows, there is often a mix of these categories in the same waters, at the same time, as trout move in and out of heavily fished waters.

Uneducated trout are those that have seen few if any people in a year and are easy to catch because they probably have never experienced an angler's tricks. They are highly susceptible to most any fly or lure and are easily caught. They also spook easily and won't start feeding again for a while once spooked. Stealth is more important than exact imitation on these waters. Don't assume that just because a place is remote, the fish are uneducated. Float planes and jet boats make many remote places accessible on a daily basis and the fish can get educated quickly.

Educated trout are those that live in waters where fishing pressure is moderate or high and where harvesting fish is legal and yet somehow they have escaped human predation. They have habits that help survival, such as feeding before or after the main fishing pressure occurs, such as at night, feeding on extra-small items that are drifting naturally, feeding in secondary feeding lies, stopping their feeding when a human presence is detected or feeding only occasionally on extra-large foods such as lemmings, whitefish, lampreys or salmon flesh, which gives the angler fewer chances at catching that fish.

Catch-and-release-educated trout are becoming more and more common as regulations and sportsmen's attitudes change and angling pressure increases, even on remote waters. These fish are hooked, caught and released occasionally or often in heavily fished waters by sophisticated anglers or novices with good guides. These trout learn to accept humans into their environment. On some waters, if they quit feeding every time a human pres- ence was detected, they might starve to death. Their survival instinct won't allow that so they adapt by becoming more selective.

They reject commonly seen fly patterns, especially those that are not fished in a natural way. They don't spook as easily but do get even more selective when they know you're around. The angler notices that the fish is feeding but at the same time ignoring most of his presentations.

Natural drift or action is required, as is accurate imitations and accurate presentation and creative fishing approaches. Naturally, stealth is desired here because if they don't see or hear you, they won't get so hard to fool.

Anadromous trout are those that have very close ties to steelhead or that are indeed true steelhead. They come into the rivers from the ocean to spawn. Fish with similar habits come from large lakes such as Lake Iliamna or Naknek Lake (often called lake fish) only at certain times of the year. This migratory behavior differs from the more resident trout in that they seem to be instinctually migrating for spawning or some other purpose and not with the express purpose of feeding, but they will feed. They often travel into the rivers only in the spring or fall and are recognizable because of their grayish back and bright silver sides that are different from the dark green backs and darker colors of fish that have been in streams for weeks. The exception are spawning fish that develop richer colors as they near the spawn. Some newly arrived fish get hooked easily, just as fresh steelhead or salmon might, but once disturbed or once they settle into a comfortable run, they often get very difficult to tempt.

Like steelhead or Atlantic salmon, they might take flies more out of curiosity or as an intercept response than for feeding. Also like steelhead, the first few casts of the day are often the most productive, with unpredictable reactions to subsequent attempts. They are often the biggest fish in a run and anglers after truly large fish usually fish Alaska in the fall or spring hoping for one of these 5- to 25-plus-pound rainbow trout. Some anadromous fish do begin feeding on salmon flesh, lampreys, sculpins and mice and some will take smaller patterns like eggs or nymphs.

Early Summer Feeding: Streamers And Nymphs

Let's start a discussion about how Alaska trout feed throughout the season by starting at the usual trout season opener in early June. By now most trout have spawned (April and May) and the rivers are ice free and starting to drop from the spring runoff. Some fish have remained in the rivers and others have migrated back to a lake or the ocean. The salmon fry are hatching out of the gravel, where their now-dead parents spawned them the year before, and are well into their migration downstream. Other immature salmon have wintered in the lakes (smolts) and are leaving for the ocean.

In the past, this time of year has been ignored by all but the king salmon anglers and trout were seldom targeted. Anglers have finally learned that even when the salmon have not yet arrived, rainbow trout can provide incredible action.

Trout on a Bitch Creek Nymph in early July.

Rainbows that are residents in the river or lake system will line up in areas where they can ambush the downstream-migrating young salmon. The salmon fry or smolts are only an inch to 3 inches long or so but their numbers make for quite a sardine feast. These feeding spots, where the salmon fry are funneled, are usually quite concentrated with trout and many other parts of the stream are barren. Knowing where to go in early season is essential for success.

Lake inlets and outlets (especially outlets) are prime spots, as are short sections of stream between two lakes. The trout sometimes get so thick they blacken the stream bottom. Fishing is fast and furious for those who properly fish fry or smolt patterns. The salmon fry usually pass in waves and rainbows can be seen breaking the surface as they chase the fry and are often mistaken for dry-fly-feeding fish. At this time of year, rainbows are generally lean from spawning activity and a long winter but they are also strong and eager feeders. They average 12 to 26 inches in many areas and some will go to 30 inches or more.

Egg patterns work in early June for some fish. These fish are the ones that have spawned or still recognize the eggs as a food source. Some might even eat them because of faded imprints they have of the previous year's salmon-egg banquet. Use orange or amber eggs to imitate trout eggs and fluorescent fire orange or pink ones for salmon eggs.

Alaskan style streamers often work very well in June. Just remember that some trout are totally keyed into salmon fry but others are opportunistic and will take almost anything that looks like a meal. Many trout have survived the winter by feeding on minnows, sculpins, salmon smolts, leeches and lampreys they might find in the lakes, so they are still conditioned to feeding on a variety of large edibles.

Salmon smolts are the salmon fry that have wintered over in a lake and grown to two or more inches before going to sea. They are mostly available in the lower-elevation areas as they come out of lakes on their way to the ocean. You can usually find out the fry or smolt sizes by looking in the small slack-water areas near shore where they might rest or feed. Some trout get very selective to size so streamers the right length and bulk are critical.

Some streams provide lamprey eels with spawning substrate and larger trout will feed on these active swimmers. Common colors are black, dark purple and gold, with a pink sucker-mouth. They are best fished in the deeper runs and drop-offs where they might be migrating through and where large trout can intercept them. They are part of the reason that trout take black, purple or yellow streamers, (i.e., Egg Sucking Leeches).

15

Lake trout (mackinaw) will move out of lakes and take up feeding positions in moving water to feed on salmon fry or smolts. They usually prefer slower water than the rainbows and are often concentrated in the just-barely-moving water at the inlets and outlets of lakes and can provide some interesting streamer fishing.

Char (Arctic char or Dolly Varden) also take up feeding lies in many rivers and mix somewhat with the trout as they feed on the plentiful food source.

Nymphs are also very productive, whether they are imitations or attractors. The hatches in Alaska are sometimes unpredictable but, generally speaking, the same places that have trout stacking up for a salmon fry meal also

Sculpin and imitation. Sculpins are available in many rivers and are a favorite food of large trout.

have some hatches in June and early July and therefore some nymphs are available to the trout. Some trout get focused in on the fry and others are very receptive to nymph and dry-fly imitations.

Most of Alaska's aquatic hatches occur sometime in June or early July and a few places see small hatches again in late summer and early fall. Some years the hatches are going when the season starts but most wait till mid-June. Mayflies, caddis, stoneflies, midges and black flies all hatch off in selected areas and times. Alaska isn't well known for its dry-fly fishing because most people that visit Alaska do so during the salmon runs and most of Alaska's insects have adapted to hatching off before the salmon begin digging their nests or in areas separate from salmon activity.

I was lucky enough to have guided on the Copper River (Iliamna area) from Chris Goll's Rainbow River Lodge.

Gold, purple and black lampreys are common in Alaskan streams and lakes and often fall prey to large trout.

This river is known as having some of the best dry-fly fishing in Alaska as well as limited access due to private native ownership. It produces thousands of rainbows in the 14- to 26-inch range on dry flies. The large brown stoneflies hatching would bring up the biggest fish, sometimes to 30 inches or more. Other rivers I guided or floated have good hatches as well, including Green Drakes.

Salmon fry like to migrate during low light periods so sometimes the fry fishing gets slow mid-day on sunny days and trout will turn to nymphs and dry flies if available. My clients have often experienced excellent dry-fly fishing in the afternoons in areas below the stillwater sections of lake outlets. A mixed bag of rainbow trout, grayling and smaller char are available in some waters and can be caught on dry flies.

On one outlet stream I fished regularly, there was always good attractor dry-fly fishing (Royal Wulffs etc.) during windy days. It took me a while to figure out the fish weren't just hitting attractors for fun. They were eating the

Bullethead Brown Stonefly with natural.
Hatches like this bring up big trout in early summer.

fuzz blown off the streamside willows. Small, off-white willow-fly larvae built fuzzy cocoons out of willow seed fuzz and on windy days these were blown onto the water. Trout were taking the white-winged dry flies for these fuzz-covered morsels.

Even when traditional aquatic insects are not present, aquatic Diptera species, usually called black flies or black gnats, hatch off in great numbers. I like to think of them simply as fat midges. Trout, and especially grayling, like these insects so small, dark dry flies work well in the flats and tailouts. Although grayling and trout to 22 inches are the usual catch on dries, sometimes you're pleasantly surprised by a 24- to 30-inch rainbow, char or lake trout.

Alaskan mayfly.

Trout spread out quickly as salmon fry numbers dwindle and the nymph and dry-fly action increases. By late June, the outlets areas have a normal complement of trout spread all through the areas where they can find food. They always seem to prefer certain water types and will group up there but the groups are not nearly as big as those seen during the salmon fry migration. Some trout move back to the lakes and wait for the salmon. Others will feed on whatever is available in their streams. Some tagged fish have shown that they actually leave the rivers and lakes, go to the ocean, and then go up other rivers, following salmon runs.

Generally speaking, king salmon are the only salmon to be found in some trout waters in June. On rivers that support both, you can get into these huge, fresh salmon and also the trout, char and grayling. Although some of the trout are large, they have not yet bulked up on the salmon eggs that will be available later.

Mid-summer: Nymphs, Dries and Streamers

Nymph, dry-fly and streamer action continues into July. Before the sockeye salmon and other salmon get there, trout feed pretty much like their southern cousins and if you like traditional trout techniques, come to Alaska before the sockeye salmon begin running in early July. Some rivers also have big runs of chum and pink salmon.

Once the salmon arrive, the trout are not the same. Sockeye salmon have particularly heavy runs in trophy trout waters. Once they arrive in numbers, the salmon push the trout out of the holes and into the skinny water behind them. The salmon make the trout spooky and nervous but this situation also provides the angler with some excellent fishing opportunities. Some trout stay around the perimeters of the salmon but are nervous, as waves of large salmon push them around, and will eventually retreat to the water where salmon aren't holding.

The fresh salmon are bright silver and full of fight. Many anglers plan their trip to coincide with these fresh salmon runs so they can take home a few fillets from their trip. It's not uncommon to catch and release 5 to 50 or more salmon in a day and they can give you all the action you

Nice rainbow from the Copper River.

Overview: Big jumping rainbows like this one give memories that last forever.

Nymphing for fresh sockeye salmon is fun and productive. A natural drift and quick reactions are necessary to set the hook when the salmon gently and quickly crushes the fly.

want. Most anglers get salmon fever and forget all about the trout. A mistake, I think.

The trout seem to get a late start on feeding activity now so fish for salmon in the mornings and then scale down your tackle and go for trout in the afternoon. Salmon prefer to migrate in low light periods and often hole up on sunny days. The trout get less nervous as migrations slow and then begin feeding better. Because they are in the shallow-water riffles, they are often easily sight-fished with medium or small nymphs and dry flies. Stealth is important because the trout are still somewhat nervous and spook easily. You can often have great sight-fishing for 16- to 30-inch trout in water two feet deep or less. Just remember that the trout are moody so you should concentrate on salmon when the trout don't seem to be feeding.

Hatches still occur now and they are recognized by the trout, attractor or natural dry flies often produce well in the afternoon.

Streamers still work well but the streamer action slows a little, especially if the water is low and clear. Nymphs and dry flies work well until the salmon eggs start rolling.

The salmon begin to change into their spawning colors, pair off and begin digging and defending their nests. The salmon are great game fish up until they actually begin spawning, even after they turn color.

Some of the fastest egg fishing for rainbows I've seen has been during this time. Trout that have been nervous and sometimes difficult to catch suddenly go nuts for the much-anticipated salmon eggs. There is also an influx of trout in some waters. They follow the salmon like a puppy following a bone and eat the eggs the salmon drop before spawning and the eggs that become lost to the current during the spawn.

The trout stay in the shallow riffles where the salmon begin spawning and in the drop-offs just below spawning areas. They load up on the new food supply. The salmon knock nymphs loose from the gravel, the trout will eat them but they prefer eggs to anything else. Trout feed on eggs voraciously and will soon give up all desire to eat other foods.

Late Summer: The Egg Season

This egg-fishing period is very important to the trout. It provides them with a much-needed boost in food volume and energy. The trout have incredible growth in a short period of time. An egg-feeding trout can go from 5 to 8 pounds in just over a month. Trout anglers need little more than a small box of various egg patterns because by late July through August until early September they eat eggs almost exclusively (not everywhere, however, some trout areas where salmon densities are lower you'll see trout continuing to feed on standard patterns).

Some fly anglers don't like egg fishing and others live for it, it's a matter of personal preference. I like it because many of the trout are highly visible and sight-fishing in the clean gravel runs and riffles is very intriguing. It's as close to hunting as fly-fishing can get. You can spot and pick out large individual fish, stalk them and fish to them.

Trout that were originally eating anything that looks remotely like an egg soon get very selective. Egg density increases until there is literally a carpet of eggs rolling down the river bottom and swirling in the back-eddies. Educated trout in catch-and-release waters get especially selective and the egg's size and color are very important as is a natural and accurate drift. The angler looks for trout that are holding behind the spawning salmon. Almost everywhere there is a big pod of spawning salmon, there will also be some trout holding just below them or mixed in with them, feeding heavily on drifting eggs. When the egg concentration is the thickest, trout will hold on the drop-offs and deeper runs downstream of large groups of spawning salmon. When egg density decreases the trout move in behind the individual spawning salmon still left in riffles and runs. Because of the food density during egg season, trout can sit in fast-water chutes and still gain much more energy than they expend.

In little-fished waters, trout will accept many egg patterns. Patterns like the ever popular Glo Bug work well for these trout. Iliamna Pinkies evolved in the Iliamna Lake region and they work well for all but the most selective fish. Other patterns like the Silicone Egg, Nuke, Halo Egg, Bead Egg, Crystal Egg or Goey Egg have their place and work well at times. Bead Eggs have become very popular with lodge guides in the last few years.

If the trout seem to be ignoring your egg pattern, try other colors, sizes or styles. Keep switching and often you will find the best pattern, size and color for the day. Egg color can often be more critical than size. Natural colors like pink or fluorescent orange should be your first choice but at times, attractor colors like chartreuse or cerise catch the attention of fish better. Hooks should be short shank, wide gape, extra-strong and very sharp.

The water can get murky from so many salmon spawning at once. Trout are harder to spot but fishing can still be fairly good.

When the trout turn selective, a smaller hook should be used.

The salmon in some rivers are so numerous the spawning fish make the river murky just from their sheer numbers digging up nests in the stream bottom. When that happens, there are usually so many eggs that the trout get full and either stop feeding or become extra selective. There is literally a flowing carpet of salmon eggs on the stream bottom and it's no wonder the trout become difficult to catch, not only are they full but they have so much to choose from, why would they take yours out of all the others available? Fear not, accurate presentations still produce well at times.

Trout will jump clear of the water, taunting you, as if they are happy and full for once during the year and they jump out of sheer exuberance. The theory is that the trout jump to break up the eggs inside them so they can be digested easier. Jumping trout are notoriously difficult to catch but will sometimes respond to accurate, repeated presentations. The trout also require very exact egg patterns like the Dipped Bead Egg.

Spotting trout might be difficult due to the murkiness caused by excessive spawning but the fact that most of the salmon are red and the trout have an olive gray/green back can help. The newest rainbow arrivals are mostly silver and are very difficult to see so once you discover the water type the trout prefer, work the water carefully, even if you can't spot trout. You'll often be surprised by a chromer on the end of your line.

Pacific salmon spawn, then die. There are no exceptions. The carnage present this time of year can be incredible. The Iliamna Lake region, for example, gets about 22

Trout go nuts for the first salmon eggs of the season.

million sockeye salmon. The shores and back-eddies get littered with their bodies and bears are often seen roaming the banks for easy meals. Bears prove to be a very small threat in trophy trout waters, despite their numbers, as long as you use some common sense and thought about how you deal with their presence. They are well fed and seldom aggressive towards humans. See Alaskan Wildlife on page 60 for more information on bears.

Silver salmon come into some rivers and many anglers time their trips to coincide so they can catch both trout and silvers, long thought to be the most fun Pacific salmon on a fly rod. Every river has its own density and mix of species and not all waters have all the species you might want to fish for, so float plane flights to different rivers might be in order. I did have two float trips, one on the Mulchatna and one on the Alagnak where I caught an Alaskan super grand-slam which is all 5 salmon species (silver, king, chum, pink, sockeye) plus rainbows, char and grayling in one day.

Loose sockeye eggs get bleached soon after they're deposited in the stream giving the eggs an easter egg effect.

It can only happen in a few rivers in late August once the silvers get there and before all the other salmon species die.

When the spawning salmon thin out, the water clears up quickly. The dead salmon might stink and many people don't understand the seeming waste. Actually, they represent natures grand design. If salmon didn't die and fertilize the river with their own bodies, the rivers they spawn in wouldn't be able to support their own offspring in the future, because of the sterile nature of many Alaska watersheds. There wouldn't be as many bears or eagles and there wouldn't be nearly as many big trout.

This massive salmon die-off marks the beginning of some of the best trout fishing of the season, if you're after a big trout and also silver salmon.

A 29-inch rainbow from Bear Creek.

Fall: Big-Trout Time

Late August, September and early October is when trophy hunters migrate to Alaska, both for trout and for big game like bear, moose and caribou. Hunters usually key in on their big game first but will often go after trout or silver salmon once their hunt is over.

As the salmon die, the abundance of eggs is reduced and trout become more susceptible to angling again. The decrease in natural food and the generally good condition of the streams make prime sight-fishing opportunities available. That doesn't mean that the trout are easy to catch. Daily catch rates are down quite a bit from those in the early summer but the average size of these rainbows is much bigger. Trout have gained most of the bulk they will have this season and are full of energy. They might also be educated from the season's fishing pressure.

The resident trout are much bigger than in spring, there are some big lake fish that came in with the salmon and some huge fall-run rainbows are beginning to enter the rivers. The shortening days bring a nip to the air and trout seem to know that their abundant foods are starting to run out and that winter is just around the corner.

Sight-fishing anglers use egg imitations to visible trout and even when you can't see them, they are in the prime spots (gravel depressions, gravel drop-offs and swift runs). Because there are not as many eggs to compete with yours, your chances increase. At the same time, the fish can be difficult to catch unless you use ultra-accurate egg imitations and accurate presentations.

Dead salmon begin decaying and trout have a taste for salmon flesh. Salmon catch on midstream snags or rocks in swift streams and the current pulls chunks of flesh and unspawned eggs from the salmon, which the trout eat.

Trout are often found behind these "salmon-catching snags" so it's worth a few casts even if you can't spot trout. On slower streams, the salmon roll across the bottom in the currents and their decaying flesh breaks up into smaller pieces. Look for back eddies full of dead salmon and fish parallel and just downstream. The size of salmon-flesh flies you fish should be adjusted to water type, large sizes for fast water with snags and small sizes for slower water.

Once the flesh feeding starts (September), streamer fishing also heats up again and proportionately increases as egg availability is reduced. Leech, lamprey, sculpin and mouse imitations work well again along with egg and flesh patterns.

As previously mentioned, some hatches occur after the salmon die and dry-fly or nymph action occurs in limited areas, usually on smaller waters or where salmon spawning

Green Drake on the Ongivinuk River.

The author on Little Bear Creek.

*Healthy, clean rainbow that
recently came upriver from a large lake.*

has not dug up the whole stream bottom (where the stream bottom is still dark colored from moss). It attracts mostly small trout, grayling and char but can include large trout.

As water temperatures fall and river food becomes scarce, trout move out of the riffles and into the deeper holes and runs again and many begin slowly migrating downstream to the lakes or lower river areas where they will winter. As always, their movements parallel the concentrations of food. Streamers are productive but are generally not fished fast. The cold water keeps the trout from wanting to chase too much and streamers are generally just swung in the current with little action or drifted along the bottom like a nymph. There are exceptions, so experiment with retrieves.

Most wilderness lodges that cater to fly anglers close in late September or early October. They don't want to get frozen in and few anglers want to battle the harsh weather often associated with this time of year. Snow, wind, below-freezing air temperatures and cold water temperatures keep all but the hardiest anglers off the streams. The fishing is good for dedicated anglers until ice-up and some warm fall years give the few anglers around access to uncrowded waters and very large trout. Cold water keeps the trout sluggish, until hooked, so slow, deep presentations are most productive. Assume the fish have a small strike zone, get the fly as close to the fish's nose as possible. You might have to deal with ice flows in the rivers as overnight ice breaks up in the day.

The upper sections of rivers are often abandoned by the trout, except areas near large lakes. By ice-up most of the trout are gone from the smaller, more sterile spawning

Beautiful Alaskan rainbow caught on the famous Wiggle Bug.

streams. Those few that stay are usually chased out in the spring when ice flows become severe, then they enter again to spawn or feed on fry.

There are certain waters that are open year-round or are open for a spring season, before spawning and spring runoff. Since regulations change according to angler demand and for biological reasons pertaining to the trout, check the current regulations for those waters. There is a short period of time in the spring when some waters are fishable as the ice melts back and before the main runoff starts. Large trout can be caught then but weather and access is unpredictable so few anglers take advantage of this brief time period. Southeast Alaska has many excellent steelhead streams that are great in spring. In early June, the general trout season opens again and the cycle of trout feeding begins again.

During unseasonably warm, dry years or unusually wet, cool years, the salmon runs and the reactions of the trout may follow patterns that start earlier or later by 2 or more weeks from normal. Some years the weather actually determines how good the salmon runs will be.

A good example is the 1997 mid-summer season that saw warm temperatures and generally low, warm waters. Salmon came into the rivers a little late as they waited for cooler, higher flows, which never really came. They waited until the last minute then shot up to their spawning areas. It was supposed to be a good year for salmon density but it turned out to be a low year, due to the weather. With the salmon density down, the trout had less food and gained less weight than normal. When egg density is low like this, trout will feed on other foods through the egg season. This doesn't mean that the fishing was bad, just different than normal. 1998 saw higher than normal water and generally early to normal salmon runs. Because of a poor spawn four years previous, 2000 had low run numbers in some streams. Every year is different, take it as it comes.

III

Alaska Trout Techniques & Tackle

Nymphs, Eggs & Flesh

NYMPHING TECHNIQUES WITH NYMPHS OR EGG patterns are perhaps the most effective year-round method of hooking trout. From the season opener to its close, there is seldom a day when nymphing (or egging) doesn't work. Exceptions might be when high flows muddy the water or when fish are totally keyed in on salmon fry. There are several techniques of nymphing and all work but you will probably develop a preference.

Natural Drift

Getting a natural drift is very important much of the time, especially in regularly fished waters. Natural drift refers to the techniques that make your fly drift similarly as possible to the naturals drifting in the current. Tension on the line causes drag that looks unnatural to selective trout so to get a natural drift you must have slack in the line and leader so the flies drift naturally.

Author with 32-inch rainbow. Sight-fishing for large trout is close to trophy hunting.

The best method of accomplishing this is with a floating fly line, a strike indicator, a long leader and weights to get the fly down. Thread the indicator onto the leader and place it approximately 1 1/2 to 2 times the depth of the water you're fishing from the fly. Example: If the water is 4 feet deep, then put it 6 to 8 feet from the fly. Strike indicators can be foam, cork or yarn but should be buoyant enough to stay afloat during the drift, until acted upon by a fish. Tippet size for nymphs and eggs varies from 4X to 1X.

Weight the leader 18-30 inches from the fly with split shot heavy enough to get the fly near the bottom for much of the drift. Varying the amount of weight you use and the distance of the indicator to the fly is critical. When you change water types or depths, change the rig as well.

The basic technique goes like this: Cast up and across, far enough upstream to give the fly time to sink before reaching the fish. Keep plenty of slack on the water for a natural drift. If the line starts to belly in the current, mend it up or downstream to compensate, immediately after mending, put more slack line on the water to lengthen the natural drift. Watch the indicator for hesitations, twitches and any unnatural movements that might indicate that a fish has the fly. Set the hook quickly if you think there is a fish on. Let the indicator movement trigger your arm to strike, otherwise you might miss the fish by waiting too long. This is especially critical during egg season or when fish are selective. They can spit the fly out extremely fast. At the end of the drift, if no fish takes the fly, pick the rig up out of the water and cast it back upstream. Repeated presentations to get the perfect drift into a small strike zone are often required to hook large fish.

Bounce Rigs

Bounce rigs are designed to use extra weight so that the weight and fly bounce along the bottom through much of the drift. Obviously this technique works best on clean gravel runs, not in snag-filled areas. One bounce rig uses floating line and a long leader, 4X to 1X tippet and split-shot 18 to 30 inches from the fly. The strike indicator is optional because you keep more tension on the line and usually feel if the line is stopped by a fish or the stream bottom. Its main advantage is that it keeps the fly on the bottom through most of the drift. On the downside, it requires more weight than the standard indicator rig which makes casting more difficult and snags up easily. Use a lob cast.

Another bounce rig uses weight on the very bottom of the leader and a dropper fly about 18 inches up from the weight. The weight is also fished right on the bottom but the fly is suspended up off the bottom. I prefer this bounce technique because I experience less snags and fewer false strikes. The optional indicator is placed about three times the water depth from the weight so you can better gauge the

drift. Mend upstream to slow the drift or allow the line to belly to speed it up if the weights drag too much. It's also a difficult rig to cast because of the weight so use a lob cast instead of the regular false casts.

A new line called the Deep Nymphing Line (available through Cortland and other manufacturers) is a thin, floating shooting line (.022") that is rigged with the weight on the bottom with a dropper system. When using this rig we call it "extreme nymphing" because it can get you down in those big deep runs where other techniques fail. The cast is a pendulum cast (8 feet of line swung behind the rod) that loads the rod (with a single haul) and then the line is shot almost like on a spinning rod. It can get you far into a river where a backcast is impossible and will keep the fly down deep for a long distance. Keep the rod tip high and feel the weights bounce along the bottom. Then set the hook when the line stops. It's unconventional but extremely effective on the deep, swift gravel runs and holes of Alaska's rivers. The feel allows you to set the hook more quickly than strike indicator methods. Use a large stripping basket with cones (to help prevent line tangles) for best results.

Sinking Line

Although sinking lines seem natural for sinking fly techniques, they actually hinder you from getting a natural drift with nymphs. There are times, however, when nymphs on a slow swing on a sinking line will work well. In pocket water, you can plunk a weighted fly, short leader (2-6 feet long) and fast-sinking line (sink-tip or full-sink) in behind rocks, logs or deep drop-offs. It's often known as the Charlie Brooks Method for his book called *Nymph Fishing For Larger Trout.*

First, let the rig sink deep, then when close to the bottom, keep a slight tension by raising or lowering the rod slowly so you can keep contact with the fly. Let it drift through the pocket or hole by following it with the rod and allow it to raise or swing on the end of the drift. The take will be felt as a tightening of the line or as a tap. Other times the fish will literally rip line out of your hands. Although this technique has been known to catch many big trout, it is not as effective on educated catch-and-release trout (with nymphs) because it doesn't allow a very natural drift. It is, however, a very effective attractor nymph and streamer technique in fast pocket water.

Streamers, Leeches & Mice

The cold air, big streamers and oversize trout seemed to go hand in hand for some reason on this nasty fall day. Frost covered the gravel bars and froze the damp sand, including the brown bear footprints. The dark, windy sky threatened snow. The air was surprisingly fresh because the frost had stopped the dead salmon carnage from stinking. My fingers were a little chilly but the rest of me was fine because of the poly and fleece layering system I had under my breathable waders. Besides, every cast was full of a warming expectation. Several large trout had already succumbed to the magnum size 2 Wiggle Bug and I could feel it working in the current with each swing.

There was a slight tap, which indicated that a trout was following and bumping the fly with his nose. Senses tingled with heightened awareness...another small bump which was followed by a smashing strike that ripped line from my hand. No need to set the hook, just concentrate on letting the slack line hit the reel without tangling. The huge trout broke water on a slashing jump that took it five feet, against the drag, through the air. It was a big fish, well over 10 pounds and it started peeling line and backing off the reel, going upstream.

The huge 'bow then did the tug of war they're so famous for, threatening to break the 1X tippet as it spun, surged and made numerous runs into the backing. By keeping side pressure on the fish with the 8-weight rod and letting the fish work against the smooth disc drag of the reel, the fish eventually tired. Twenty minutes after the hookup and 200 yards downstream, it rolled over and ceded the battle. My fishing companion was upstream doing battle with a fish of his own so I laid the rod next to the fish in shallow water and took a picture. The fish went from the rod butt almost to the first stripping guide, and it was fat. Streamers did their job again!

For truly big fish, nothing beats streamer season. The trout of Alaska are very opportunistic and none more so than the extra-large ones. There are two basic streamer seasons, as already described. One is from the time the season opens until the salmon eggs get thick and the other is from when the eggs thin out in early fall until the waters freeze over. Streamers also work season-long in areas not frequented by salmon, such as some lake trout and char areas. There is no such thing as a streamer technique that does not work but there is always one technique that works better than others on a particular day, so here are a few options for you to try.

Classic Swing

The classic swing is the same technique you might use wet-fly fishing, steelhead or Atlantic salmon fishing. You cast across or down-and-across and simply let the fly swing in the current. If nothing hits or chases the fly, you take a step downstream and repeat. Work completely through a run in this manner. Twitching the fly with your line hand as it swings is a good variation, to give it some life and swimming or breathing action. If deep water or some other obstacle is in your way, gradually lengthen your line with each cast instead of taking a step or two.

Traditionally, this technique was done with neutrally buoyant silk lines, more commonly now it's done with floating fly lines. It also works extremely well with fast-sinking sink-tip or sink-head fly lines, to help keep the fly deeper. My favorite lines are the 13- to 30-foot sinking-head steelhead lines that are available now such as Cortland's QD lines or Jim Teeny's T-series lines. As with most streamer techniques, tippet size seldom matters, just as long as it's strong. 0X to 3X is a common tippet size and use long leaders (7-12 feet long) for floating lines, with weighted flies. Use short leaders (1 to 6 feet long) with sinking lines. Ultra-clear water and educated fish may require 9-foot 3X streamer leaders on sinking lines.

My sinking-line leaders are seldom more than a 12-inch butt section with a loop to which I tie a 2- to 3- foot section of heavy tippet, using an improved clinch knot. For all my streamers, I use the non-slip mono loop knot which gives you 100% knot/line strength, if tied properly.

This technique (with variations) is the most commonly used method to fish Woolly Buggers, Wiggle Bugs, Marabou Muddlers, fry and smolt imitations, Bunny Bugs and so forth. It's easy to do and it works well from shore, a wading position or from an anchored boat.

Dead Drift

When fish are not coming up to the classic swing, you must go down to them with a dead drift near the bottom. Cast across or up-and-across and allow the streamer to sink near the bottom. Wiggle some line out and mend downstream if necessary to keep the fly down near the bottom. At the end of the drift, let the fly swing up. "Dead drift" is a slight misnomer because there is always some tension on the line that gives the fly some action and you give the fly slight twitches as you mend and let line out. Watch for a flash or a tightening of the line during the drift and set the hook. When the line tightens, it's either the bottom or a fish.

This technique is very effective with soft, flowing streamers that use marabou or rabbit fur but also works well with fry, smolt, sculpin, flesh or rubber-leg nymph patterns. Eggs can be fished this way as well but are usually best fished with a floating line and split-shot technique. Because of the size of most streamers and the chance at big trout, a 6- to 8- weight rod is recommended with all streamer techniques.

Streamer Retrieves

Streamers imitate various minnows, young salmon, eels, sculpin, etc. and so the fly should look like a swimming, frightened, injured or dead fish (or parts thereof). Try to

Streamer box on a streamside Alaskan flower bed.

Streamer angler.

imagine what the natural might be doing and use a streamer technique and retrieve that might imitate it well.

When you retrieve the line, you automatically give the
fly some action. Some days the fish want little, if any,
action to the fly and sometimes the faster you strip the fly,
the crazier you drive the trout. Experimentation is clearly
called for in streamer techniques and once you find one that
produces, stick with it until it quits producing, then try
something else. Following are a few variations to try:

• Adapt the classic swing by stripping in small amounts of
  line as it swings. This gives the fly more action and
  imitates a swimming minnow. Then st rip the line straight
  upstream as it straightens below you.

• On small waters or while drift-fishing, cast across to the
  far bank and mend downstream. The streamer will swim
  downstream along the far bank then swing out from
  the bank.

• Retrieve straight upstream along the edges of current lines,
  after the streamer has swung across the current.

• Vary the retrieve sequence, such as three fast strips
  followed by a short pause, then several more strips,
  pause, repeat.

• Change the retrieve length and speeds, sometimes stripping slowly with short pulls, sometimes speeding up the
  strip and doing long strips as well.

• Generally speaking, in fast water, let the current impart
  much of the action to the fly. In slower water, retrieves
  become more important.

•Tease the fly in front of fish that don't seem to be interested. Sometimes they will get nervous or irritated and strike out at your fly.

•Long, slow strips followed by a pause work very well with front-weighted flies (lead eye, etc.). It creates a jigging action that looks like the up-and-down movements of a minnow.

•Sometimes vertical movement is more important than horizontal. I've experienced days when the trout only took weighted flies on the drop (sink) and ignored swimming flies.

•Trout often try to stun their prey before fully grabbing it, so don't set the hook until there is more substance than just a tap, you'll hook more trout.

Surface Critters

When trout are aggressive and opportunistic, surface patterns often work well. I'm referring to surface streamers, not dry flies. These include unweighted Muddler Minnows, mouse and lemming patterns, skimming flies like Bombers, poppers, etc. The season is much the same as general streamer season, early and late. When dialed in on eggs, they generally ignore these critters.

Look for areas where there are undercut banks or drop-offs. Cast the fly as close to the opposite bank as possible. One foot is often too far. Streamers and mice tied weedless are nice because you can put them right into the grass or rocks of the far shore and twitch them off and into the water. You will miss more trout using weed guards, however, so accurate casting technique is more desirable.

Trout can feel and hear streamers and will come to investigate even if they can't see them right away. They hear the splat as it hits the water, they feel the pressure waves as you pull it through or across the water. They hear the bubbles and slurping noises as the streamer or mouse surges across the top. The fly interacting with air, water and the meniscus (rubbery surface of the water) gives the trout a true sensory delight. Unrstrained curiosity and a quick opportunistic lunge often is the result.

Twitch the fly enticingly across the water surface. Make your mouse or minnow pattern swim like the natural it's designed to imitate. For mice, keep the rod tip high as you twitch the fly, to keep it on the surface. Even subsurface mice patterns catch trout, however. I have also done well with mice patterns during the stonefly hatches on some rivers. They will take it as a fluttering stone. Fish it like an egg-laying caddis at times. Jiggle the rod tip enough to skitter the fly, then drop the rod and let it drift. Another technique is to strip the fly hard and fast, making it go under water, leaving a trail of bubbles then pop back to the surface on the pause. They can also be dead drifted on

the surface, if the fish hears the plop, it may come to investigate, much like grasshopper fishing.

Dry Flies

Although Alaska is not famous for its hatches, there are enough aquatic insects to get the trout interested at certain times and places, sometimes with a big hatch. Nearly all streams have some combination of mayfly, caddis, midge, blackfly or stonefly hatches.

Natural Drift

Drifting dry flies naturally with the current is usually the most effective dry-fly technique. If you observe fish feeding on the surface, first try to determine what hatch is occurring. If you can't see anything, it might be midges or black flies. If rising fish ignore your dry flies, they are either very selective or are feeding on salmon fry at the surface. Trout often switch to insects mid-day when the salmon fry are not migrating. Since this is early season, attractor flies like Royal Wulffs are often appropriate and effective as fish haven't developed selectivity yet. If the hatch lasts more than a couple days or if fishing pressure is high, the trout may get very selective, which should suggest more exact imitations of the dominant insect.

To get a natural drift, use a floating line with a long tapered leader and a tippet of 5X to 3X. Cast upstream of the trout and allow the line and leader to land on the water with enough slack so it drifts naturally with the current as it passes the trout. Repeat if the trout does not respond. Sometimes their strike zone or feeding lane is small and your fly must pass closely to be taken.

Dry-Fly Swing

Although natural drift is usually more desirable, there are times when a dry fly swung in the current will do better. Caddis, gnat hatches and sometimes stonefly hatches create opportunities for you to swing the dry fly in the current to imitate the egg-laying antics of adult insects. Vary the way it swings. Often, all you need to do is cast down and across and let the fly swing on its own in the current. If caddis or stoneflies are laying eggs, try skittering the fly upstream by raising the rod, then drop the rod and allow the fly to drift naturally, then repeat the skitter.

Lake Techniques

You will have opportunities to fish lakes for variety or for species that are less likely to be found in rivers. One problem with lakes is that most have vast areas of few or no fish and finding concentrations of fish can be tricky as fish migrate. If the fish are land-locked, they will often be on the small side. The exceptions are when baitfish or crustaceans are plentiful or in some lowland lakes where leeches and insects abound.

Arctic char and lake trout are common in some lakes, northern pike in others. Trout and char may have a mix of resident populations that never leave the lake and some that follow the salmon fry and eggs feasts. You'll usually find the biggest concentrations of fish at inlets or outlets of lakes. Even relatively small streams entering lakes can attract small fish that feed on the insects being washed into the lake, which in turn attracts predators looking for the small fish. This should suggest the use of streamers as a primary search tool in big lakes. When several streams enter a section of lakeshore, the area between the streams is also good to try. Lake outlets are especially good during the fry migrations and again in the fall when lake trout group up to spawn. Cover the water with a sink-tip line and streamers if you're fishing from shore. Full-sink lines are better if you fish from a boat, float tube or kick-boat.

Using a sidefinder fish graph will help locate shoreline cruisers from a boat. Some large natural lakes have very large rainbow trout that cruise the shorelines looking for leeches, lampreys and minnows. The best shorelines are usually near or between streams. Islands, rocky drop-offs and the deep edge of weed beds are also good spots.

Some lakes near towns are stocked regularly and can provide trout fishing similar to lakes in the lower 48. Try to determine which insects or minnows are most prevalent and adjust your patterns and presentations accordingly.

Playing & Releasing Fish

Since you'll likely catch many fish in Alaska, you have the responsibility to release the trophy trout properly. Remember that these trout are often over 10 years old and mishandling them can cause their death, even if they're released. Guidelines for proper fish release are as follows. Play the fish as quickly as possible. A tired fish must be revived longer. When waters warm to 70 degrees or more, trout have a difficult time getting oxygen from the water and must be revived about as long as the fight. *Don't beach the fish!* Bring it into shallow water where thrashing won't hurt or dirty the fish. Touch the fish as little as possible. Use hemostats to get the hooks out easily. Barbless hooks come out more easily for unskilled releasers and the reduction in handling time is always desirable. For trout hooked with barbed hooks, press down with the hemostats to release the barb before quickly popping the hook out the way it went in.

If you want a photo, get the camera ready and photographer in position before the fight is finished so that the trout can be raised briefly, the photo taken and the fish lowered back into the water and released quickly. Don't hold the fish by the gills. Cradle the fish with both hands during the photo but don't squeeze the fish. It's especially important to support the belly of a fat fish with your hand and arm. Make sure you hold the fish over water and not land or a boat so if it wiggles out of your hands, it will be in water and not hurt on rocks, dirt or boat parts.

The best way to gently revive the trout is to pinch the lower jaw between your pointer finger and thumb, as the fish is held upright, facing upstream, in a slow current. This keeps the mouth open, water flowing over its gills and minimizes touching the trouts protective slime layer. Just release your pinch as the trout revives and powers back into the current. In lakes or other stillwater, you'll need to slide the trout through the water to move water over its gills.

Playing large fish is a skill that is easily developed in Alaska, since many of the fish are large. In the lower 48, most trout areas have few trout that will ever get you into your backing. In Alaska, it's commonplace. When you hook a large trout or salmon, make sure the hook is set properly. If you're not sure, set the hook again. The larger the hook and barb, the harder the hook must be set. Sharp hooks and small barbs make the job much easier. If the trout are large, hooks up to size 2 can be used. Smaller trout should suggest smaller hook sizes to avoid damaging the fishes eyes or other internal organs. Hooks over size 2 are illegal in some trout waters so tie your flies accordingly. Some lodges only allow clients to use hooks size 6 and smaller to help reduce trout mortality.

If you miss lots of strikes, try setting the hook low and downstream, to the side. This lets water pressure better help you set the hook. When you lose a fish, check the hook to see if it is sharp or if the point is curled slightly. The hook point should stick into your thumbnail when you drag it across at a 45-degree angle, not slip and scratch.

Trout seldom engulf streamers on the first swipe, they stun them first, then turn to leisurely eat them. If you set the hook hard on every bump, you'll miss many fish. It's better to wait for a distinct pull with weight.

Once the fish is hooked, determine if the fish will run away from you or toward you. Strip line if the fish comes toward you and make sure the line is clear of snags, your feet or the reel seat for when the fish takes out all the slack and begins ripping line off the reel. Any tangle would likely result in a broken leader and possibly a broken rod.

Don't try to stop an Alaskan fish on its first run. It's a common mistake for those not familiar with large wild fish to try to stop a fish from taking line. The result might be a broken leader or fly-line-burned fingers. Fly reels with smooth disc drags are most useful because the drags can be set before-hand. Simple click drags work but some have inadequate drag pressures and require additional "palming" of the reel to slow a fish down. A counter-balanced spool also helps reduce unwanted vibrations.

Wiggle Bugs.

Try to keep side pressure on a large fish. If it gets too far downstream you might lose the fish as it thrashes. This sometimes means you will follow a fish downstream. On exceptionally large trout and salmon, in bigger waters, having a guide with a boat or having your kick-boat handy so you can maneuver to a better position to land a fish may mean the difference between landing a really big fish or not.

Tackle & Clothing Suggestions

Alaska is known for being hard on equipment and may be responsible for more broken tackle than anywhere else. It pays to understand the things that go into a successful trip and flyfishing equipment is no exception.

Fly rods come in hundreds of varieties today and each has its place. Each species of fish and water type has its own character and ideal rod but there are general guidelines that will enable you to bring the right tackle. Rods of 8 1/2 to 9 1/2 feet long are common. Shorter rods may not allow long casts and proper line manipulation and longer rods can wear the user out because of the extra leverage and weight your arm is required to bear.

For rainbow trout and grayling fishing, a stiff action 4- to 6-weight is ideal for dry flies, nymphs, egg patterns and fry patterns. For streamers, large flesh flies, leeches, mice or for going after big rainbows in big water, a 7- or 8- weight is better to handle the heavy flies, distance casting sometimes required and the inevitable wind.

Since most anglers in Alaska will get into some salmon on a trip, an 8-weight is a good all-round salmon rod, however, for pink salmon you may wish to use your 5- or 6-weight rod and king salmon usually require a 9- to 11-weight rod. Leave your expensive bamboo rod and your ultralight rods at home, not only are they likely to

Learn about backcountry travel and you too may be rewarded.

break but they take too long to land a fish, which reduces its chances for survival when released.

Two rods are usually a minimum. One as your main rod and one as a secondary or backup rod (in case one breaks). Two primary rods and one or two backup rods are ideal. I have seen people break three rods on a trip but it's unlikely and if it does happen, someone else in your group or the lodge should have a backup rod you can borrow.

Two-piece rods are okay but for compact gear storage, many anglers are going to quality 3-, 4-, 5-, 6- or 7-piece fly rods. The new, quality rods are impaired little by the addition of the extra ferrules and allow you to transport the rod case inside a duffel bag instead of checking them separately on the airplane. They'll also fit nicely into the overhead bins, which is nice so you know that your fishing tackle will get there with you, in case your checked luggage is misdirected. I usually travel with fly rods, reels, flies, a change of clothing, lightweight waders, my coat and my camera as carry-ons. If the uncommon happens and your

luggage doesn't make it, then you'll have the hard-to-replace items with you and can rent or buy the other stuff you need.

Good, sturdy rod cases are a must for airline, auto and some boat travel. Pick one that will fit all your rods in one or duct tape several cases together securely. Always lock and duct tape the lids shut to avoid accidental or mischievous opening by machines, vibrations or persons. Some float planes have little room for long, bulky cases. Always keep rods in cloth cases during transport. If unavailable, put a thick wool sock over each end of the rods with a rubber band to keep them in place. If needed, several anglers can bundle their rod cases together to make one airline check-on instead of several.

Fly reels for Alaska need to be durable and preferably have an adjustable disc drag and counter-balanced spool. The disc drag is more versatile than the traditional click-pawl drag and counter-balanced spools keep excessive vibrations from happening when a fish is stripping line off the reel quickly. I've seen cheap reels literally explode and fall apart when matched against a big trout or salmon. The reel size should accommodate the appropriate fly line for the rod it's matched to and have 100 yards of backing (200 yards for king salmon and extra large trophy trout). One or more extra spools are desired for an extra line or two.

Fly lines are pretty basic. Floating lines are required for dry-fly, nymph, egg and fry fishing. Sink-tip lines are best for streamers, leeches, salmon flies and other flies fished subsurface on a retrieve. Ten-foot sink-tips work well on small water but usually hinge badly during a cast. Thirteen- to 30-foot sink-tips cast much more smoothly and will sink deeper when needed. Full, fast-sinking lines work for some streamer fishing in big rivers and a type I, II, III or IV full-sink line might be advisable if you're doing some stillwater fishing for rainbows, char, grayling or pike from boats. Usually two lines—the floating and sink-tip lines—will do you quite well but bring a spare just in case one gets broken, cut or shreaded.

Leaders for floating lines should be 9-10 feet long and tapered to 0X (streamers, leeches), 2X (eggs, nymphs, fry flies), 3X (eggs, dry flies), 4X, 5X (dry flies, eggs for very selective trout). Lighter leaders are generally not needed and wouldn't hold many fish anyway. Bring 0X through 5X tippet.

Neoprene or breathable membrane waders are the best choices, matched with felt-soled boots. Neoprene waders keep you warm and are buoyant in case of an accidental swim. Gore-Tex and other waterproof/breathable waders are light-weight and keep you dry when walking distances in waders (no condensation inside the waders). Insulate them with synthetic thermals and fleece. Rubber boot-foots are bulky, heavy and dangerous if you go under and are not recommended but neoprene boot-foots have their place in very cold waters. Hip boots are fine on some waters where wading is minimal. Make a habit of bringing a wader repair kit and maybe even a lightweight pair of backup waders, it can save the trip.

Layer your clothing to keep comfortable during fishing. Put moisture-transporting synthetics like polypropylene, Thermax, silk, etc. next to your skin, cover that with synthetic fleece, wool or Thinsulate clothing and have a windproof, waterproof shell over that (waders and raincoat). On colder days, another insulating layer is recommended. Avoid cotton clothing because it holds moisture, dries slowly and doesn't insulate when wet.

Wool, fleece or neoprene fingerless gloves are worth their weight in gold on cold days. A fishing hat for mild weather and a warm hat for cold weather are a must. Waders will keep your lower body dry but you need a wader rain jacket for wet weather. Waterproof, breathable fabrics are most comfortable in jackets but waterproof/non-breathable materials are fine as long as they're vented. All should have sealed, waterproof seams. A nicely tailored rain hood is a must. Polarized fishing glasses are not only practical for spotting fish better but will protect your eyes from the sun's harmful rays, poorly cast flies and from the wind. Bring two pairs. See "Planning Your Alaska Trip" section for a complete list of gear to take on various kinds of Alaska trips.

Salmon fry and Thunder Creek Special.

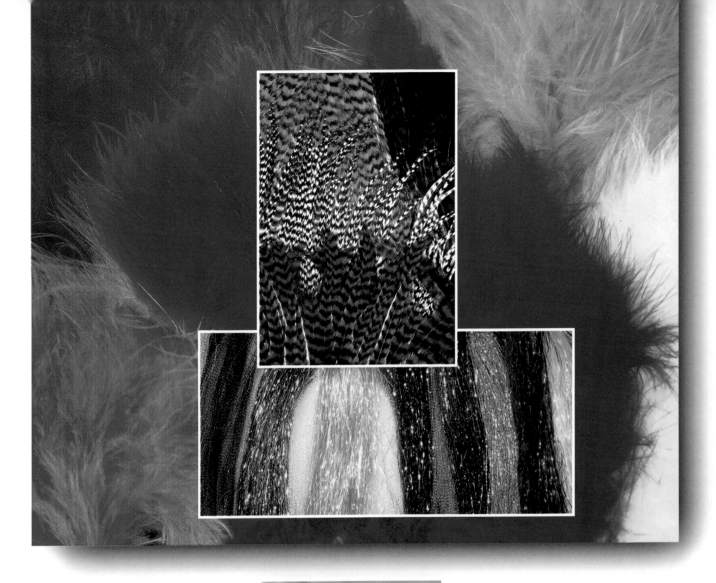

IV

Fly Patterns

ALASKA'S UNIQUE FISHERY HAS SPAWNED (forgive the pun) many new fly patterns. It's a fairly new fly-fishery if you realize that it's only been since the 70s that fly fishing has become one of the most popular and effective ways to fish Alaska. Old tackle and techniques kept most before that time dedicated to spinning, bait-casting, netting or other subsistence and commercial techniques. I credit the proliferation of quality flyfishing lodges as the main influence in the development of Alaska's new and ever-changing selection of fly patterns and techniques.

It's not uncommon for you to be waiting for a plane in a small Alaskan village and hear other passengers speaking French, German, Japanese or with an English or Australian accent. The Europeans, for example, brought a love for the Spey rod and traditional Atlantic salmon flies to Alaska. The lodges receive guests from every corner of the world and most new fly patterns have been developed by blending traditional worldwide patterns to the Alaskan experience on the tying bench after a day of fishing. The next day, the new flies are tested and the experimental fly either becomes a reject or an instant success. Guides are also constantly trying new things that might give their clients the edge in catching more fish.

Egg & Flesh Patterns

Egg imitations are more of a standard in Alaska than elsewhere, because of the abundance of spawning salmon and the incredible feeding experience it represents to trout, char

Marabou material. Top Inset: Grizzly hackle. Lower Inset: Flash material.

and grayling. Many new egg patterns are coming out lately and the old standbys still produce well. Just remember to bring two or three styles in several colors and sizes when fishing Alaska. They can work all season long. Exact representations are needed during high egg density and attractor colors are desirable for murky water or uneducated fish.

Flesh flies, although they sound repulsive, account for many large trout throughout the season, especially in September and October when salmon flesh is plentiful and egg density is reduced. Colors vary from bright orange to white. Use a size that is appropriate to the water you're fishing, one inch long for slow water and up to 4 inches long for big, fast water.

Battle Creek Specials are an eggcluster or flesh fly attractor fly tied like a Woolly Bugger and fished like a nymph or streamer.

Glo Bugs or Roe Bugs are the perennial favorite egg imitation. They have been around longer than any other single-egg imitation. They started out as a piece of synthetic tow yarn threaded into the loop on a snelled egg hook and then trimmed to shape. Now, various dyed tow yarns are used by: 1. Laying 1 to 4 strands of the poly material on top of the hook shank; 2. Using heavy thread, wrap several times over the yarn, in one place, and cinch down securely; 3. Tieing off the thread forward of the yarn; 4. Using a sharp pair of scissors, cut the yarn short (in an arc shape)

Flesh Flies. Top Row: Big Nuke (Cotton Candy), Orange Bunny Bug. Middle Row: Mini Rabbit Flesh Fly, Flesh Bunny Fly. Bottom Row: Yarn Flesh Fly, Bi-tone Flesh Fly.

Egg patterns for Alaska.

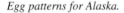

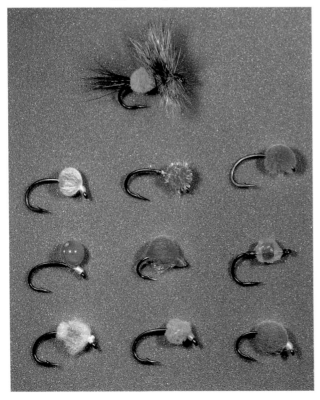

while holding the yarn strands up vertically; 5. Fluff the remaining material 360 degrees around the hook shank and trim any stray fibers into a spherical shape.

Glo Bugs, as with all eggs, are fished as you would a nymph, drifted naturally, close to the bottom of the stream, with or without a strike indicator, always with weight to get the fly down. All Glo Bug yarn colors work at times but you may want to experiment to see which attract the fish more. Fluorescent fire orange, fluorescent orange and various pinks are used often with chartreuse and cerise used for attractor colors. Peachy orange is used for imitating trout eggs.

Bead-eggs have recently become the standard fly for Alaska's bigger rainbows during salmon spawning because they so closely resemble the natural eggs. They can be so effective that some have proposed they be made illegal. Bead-eggs are simply a spherical plastic or glass bead in the appropriate diameter and color that is attached, in several ways, to the hook. Beads 6mm in diameter are used most, with 10mm, 8mm and 5mm versions also effective at times. Beads the right color and size are difficult to obtain so many tiers opt to paint their beads the appropriate color. The most effective paint technique is to: 1. Stick a fluorescent orange or red bead on a toothpick; 2. Dip it in peach, light pink, sheer or nude colored fingernail polish (pearl or regular); 3. Stick the toothpicks in Styrofoam until the polish dries; 4. Remove the beads from the toothpicks; 5. Tie them to the hook with tying thread using a loop of monofilament so they bob above the hook shank. Note: As

Bead egg components. Subtle variations in color often make a big difference in success.

real eggs fade and get bleached by the water, they turn more opaque and much lighter in color. Dipping the bead two or even three times (allowing drying time in between) can effectively imitate these bleached eggs. Spots of paint or partially dipped eggs create two tone eggs that imitate the variations often seen in nature.

Another method is to use a wide-gape hook and: 1. Stick the hook securely in a fly vise; 2. Grab the plastic bead with hemostats or needle-nose pliers; 3. Heat the front half of the hook to red hot with a lighter; 4. Quickly insert the hot hook through the bead hole and set it in place by pushing up after the hook eye emerges. This melts the plastic bead to the hook permanently. It's very durable but reduces the gape of the hook somewhat so always choose a wide-gape hook. This method is not technically legal in fly-only waters since the materials are not actually tied to the hook.

It has become common practice at lodges to simply thread a bead or two onto the leader and then tie a bare hook onto the end. This sliding bead technique is very effective but highly debatable as a true fly-fishing technique for fly-only waters. Even more effective is to pin one or two beads to the leader using toothpicks jammed

into the bead hole several inches from the hook (then break off the excess toothpick). This separates the hook from the bead and makes it look more natural to selective trout and also results in fewer missed strikes because when the bead is eaten and quickly rejected by a trout, the leader portion and the hook often remain in the fish's mouth, resulting in a hookup anyway. Many guides claim that it results in fewer lethal hookups because the hook never gets sucked deep into the gill area. All I can say is watch the Alaska sportfishing regulations for specific definitions concerning bead-egg flies. Fish according to your conscience or when being guided, let your guide be your conscience.

Iliamna Pinkies are basically a minimalist version of the Babine Special, a popular steelhead and salmon fly. They are simply a ball of chenille wrapped on a hook to create a basic spherical egg shape. The main advantage here is that it can be weighted with lead wire. 1. weight the hook with 3-4 wraps of .030" lead wire; 2. Start thread on hook and make wraps to secure the lead; 3. Tie in egg-colored chenille and wrap forward and back a couple times until a basic sphere shape is obtained and the lead is covered. Tie it off.

The color most often used is a fluorescent shell pink color but, ffluorescent red, fluorescent pink, pink, fluorescent orange, fluorescent fire orange and fluorescent chartreuse are used as well.

Nukes come in several configurations. They are basically a ball of egg-colored dubbing, chenille or a glass bead that has a halo of another material going over the nucleus so it looks like a translucent egg shell with a nucleus inside. There are many variations. Some haloes are tied front and rear and some are open at the back. They can be most effective on selective trout because they are

Various egg patterns.

Nymphs. Top Row: Bitch Creek Nymph, Mohair Leech, Peeking Caddis, Lake Midge, Chamois Caddis. Middle Row: Alaska Girdle Bug, Halfback, Woolly Worm, Zug Bug, Gold Ribbed Hare's Ear. Bottom Row: Brown Rubber Leg Stone, Bird's Nest, Flashback Pheasant Tail, Pheasant Tail, Flash Nymph.

translucent and the nucleus can be seen through the halo material. My favorite version of a Nuke, one I developed in the mid-80s, is to 1. Tie a fluorescent orange ball of dubbing or thread and a bright orange glass bead (1/8" diameter) onto a wide-gape egg or scud hook; 2. Start the thread behind the dubbing or bead and tie in about 1/3 of a strand of light pink, Alaska Roe or peach Glo Bug yarn, making sure it is 360 degrees around the hook shank; 3. Bring thread under the dubbing or bead to the front of hook shank and comb the yarn so it will flare easily; 4. Flare the yarn and bring it forward, trying to keep it 360 degrees around the nucleus bead; 5. Pull the material forward, tightly, and then push it back a small amount until it puffs up around the bead into a spherical shape and tie it off.

Hot Glue Eggs are made with hot melt glue that has been dyed an egg color. A 6mm bead of glue is created on the hook shank with a glue gun, sometimes over a glass bead nucleus. Clusters can also be made in this way.

Goey Eggs are soft plastic (rubber worm material) molded eggs that are wrapped in a one inch square of white or pink bridal veil material and tied to the hook with tying thread. They have a realistic texture that trout hold onto longer but require a "worm-proof" plastic storage devise. The chemical composition in the soft plastics will melt some plastic fly boxes. Zip-lock baggies work well. Don't use scented plastics, as with all added digestible scents, they are unacceptable in fly- and lure-only waters and might make the trout swallow the fly and be mortally injured.

Flesh Flies imitate the parts of dead and decomposing salmon flesh that have broken away from the salmon car-casses. As gruesome as it sounds, flesh becomes an important food source for trout when eggs get scarce. Most traditional flesh flies are tied with rabbit-fur strips of natural tan or white dyed peach, orange or buff on a long-shank hook. 1. Tie in a piece of stripped rabbit so the fur trails out behind like a tail; 2. Bring the thread forward and begin wrapping the fur strip forward, almost like palmering hackle, until you reach the area just behind the hook eye; 3. Tie the rabbit off securely and finish. Note: Some people prefer cross-cut strips rabbit for the body.

Micro Flesh Flies can be tied using a 1/4- to 1/2-inch strip of rabbit lashed to an egg or scud hook. The same color rabbit can be used as dubbing if desired. Use these on slower-moving streams and for more selective trout than the larger versions. I often like to alternate between peach and orange to give each fly a two-tone effect.

Yarn Flesh Flies are tied as a variation of Nukes and are often called Nukes. 1. Weight streamer hook with lead and tie a strip of orange, peach, chartreuse or pink Glo Bug yarn in, as you would a tail; 2. Tie in similar color chenille and wrap as a body to front of hook; 3. Tie in another strip of yarn as a wing and finish. This fly is used throughout the season but mostly August through October. It is an attractor pattern as well as a flesh imitation. It can be fished as an egg cluster, flesh or as a streamer.

Nymph Patterns

Bird's Nests are good stonefly imitations but work as a fry imitation as well so they are valuable from the season opener through July.

Bitch Creek Nymphs can turn the trick on fish that have seem to have lockjaw. It's a good attractor pattern that the fish may take for a leech, minnow, stonefly or lamprey.

Brown Rubber-leg Nymphs are a great imitation of the large brown stoneflies that certain rivers have in abundance and will also imitate a leech.

Flashback Pheasant-tails are great attractor patterns for early season trout and will work until the eggs become thick and often again after the eggs disperse.

Flash Body Nymphs are similar to Disco Midges but are tied mayfly style with a pearlescent flash body, peacock thorax and a brown or black hackle. With a red or pink underbody, it is a nymph that sometimes works during the egg season.

Girdle Bugs, like Bitch Creek Nymphs and Brown Rubber-legs, are good early season nymphs that imitate various species and will work again in late season, after the eggs disperse.

Gold Ribbed Hare's Ears are one of the best suggestive patterns of all time because they imitate so many foods. It's a pattern everyone should have in their boxes. We've even landed many sockeye salmon on Hare's Ears and strike indicators.

Halfbacks are a good pattern in lakes where dragonflies exist, and are a fair stonefly and a good attractor nymph because of the peacock and brown combos.

Maggots should be in your box in late season when rotten salmon carcasses get washed back into rising rivers. A Chamois Caddis works both as a maggot and a caddis larva for fishing the hatches in late June.

Tube Midges work well for lake feeding fish and for trout and grayling feeding on midges, mosquitos or black fly larvae in rivers.

Peeking Caddis are a good cased caddis larva imitation for early season use.

Woolly Worms can be fished as a nymph, streamer, leech or dry fly. It's also a good attractor fly because of the thousands of variations in body and hackle color.

Zug Bugs are an all-time favorite attractor for lakes and some rivers. The Prince Nymph also has the fish-catching features of the best attractors.

Streamers, Leeches & Mice

Alaskan Smolts should be in every angler's fly box from April through July. It imitates the larger salmon fry that may have wintered over a year or two in a lake and are now migrating to the ocean.

Alevins are the little brother to smolts and fry. They imitate the freshly hatched salmon or trout fry that trout regularly feed on in spring and early summer. There are many variations but most should be tied very sparsely and have prominent eyes and an egg sack.

Bunny Bugs are the workhorses of Alaska. I've caught almost all of Alaska's species on them. They're tied in white, pink, fuchsia, peach, tan, orange, yellow, brown, olive, purple, black and gray to imitate egg clusters, salmon flesh, minnows, sculpins, fry, lampreys and leeches. The end is tied in as a tail and the rest is wound forward like a palmered hackle. An Iliamna Pinkie-style egg-head can be placed ahead of any color body to make them "Egg Sucking Bunny Bugs". My personal favorites have one color of rabbit hackle for the body another color for the face and a few strands of flash in the tail and wing. Palmering thin strips of rabbit over crystal chenille is another way to get some flash and a good way to imitate sculpins (with a flared wool head).

Crazy Charlies are traditional bonefish flies that make great imitations of salmon fry or trout fry. Grizzly hackles on each side or black permanent marking pens make the parr marks commonly seen on salmon fry. As with most fry

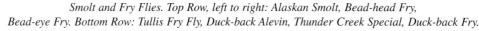

Smolt and Fry Flies. Top Row, left to right: Alaskan Smolt, Bead-head Fry, Bead-eye Fry. Bottom Row: Tullis Fry Fly, Duck-back Alevin, Thunder Creek Special, Duck-back Fry.

Streamers. Left Column, top to bottom: Purple Egg Sucking Leech, Alaskan Smolt, Wiggle Bug, Mouse Rat, Battle Creek Special. Middle Column: Bunny Matuka, Woolhead Sculpin, Black Egg Sucking Bunny Matuka, Kiwi Muddler, White Egg Sucking Bunny Matuka. Right Column: Woolly Bugger, Matuka, Zonker, Marabou Muddler, Muddler Minnow.

patterns, keep them sparsely dressed. This is another fly that can be used for sockeye salmon too.

Dave's Mouserats are so realistic they inspire confidence in their use. Trout take them for mice, lemmings, shrews, fluttering stoneflies and minnows. They are very fun to fish but trout get used to them quickly and they'll stop working if fished too often to the same fish. Sometimes large ones work, other times small ones are better.

Egg Sucking Zonkers are very similar to Bunny Bugs in form and function but have a flashy tubing body that works well for rainbows, char and lake trout. Popular colors are white, black, purple, brown and olive but most colors work at different times and places.

Kiwi Muddlers are a good variation of the standard Muddler, an all-time favorite streamer pattern. Marabou Muddlers and Lohr's Flashfire Muddlers are other variations.

Matukas are a durable and effective minnow and sculpin imitations but have been largely replaced by the Bunny patterns. Using webby dyed grizzly hen or rooster saddle gives it a barred effect not readily obtainable with rabbit strips. As with most Alaska streamers, they can be tied egg-sucking fashion. A great variation is the Rabbit Matuka, which has a rabbit strip substitute for the wing.

Marabou Muddlers are great for larger trout when searching for unseen fish or when fishing high, murky water. They also take occasional salmon species, char and steelhead. The wing color varies (white, black, brown, olive, yellow, orange). Dyed or white deer-hair heads are other variations.

Mohair Leeches are good in the lakes for trout that cruise weed beds and rocky shelves looking for leeches, *Daphnia* clusters, damselfly nymphs, dragonfly nymphs or minnows. Its suggestive style makes it a winner when fished ultra slow at times and like a regular streamer at other times. Canadian brown, Canadian blood and pond olive are all good colors. Try them naturally drifted for fresh sockeye salmon.

Thunder Creek Specials have proven their worth for fishing the fry migrations in early summer. Most are tied sparsely in smaller sizes (1-2 inches long total).

Tullis Salmonoid Frys were developed to better imitate the salmon fry to take selective trout. The dark head, eyes, barred wing and flash body have fooled many trout. They can also be tied with bead-chain or x-small lead eyes.

Wiggle Bugs are a unique pattern I invented that mimics the swimming motion of minnows, leeches, lampreys and other foods. In addition, they are good attractor flies that have taken every gamefish species in Alaska. Think of them as a Woolly Bugger that swims in a serpentine fashion. And yes, they are a hand-tied fly, not a molded, manufactured lure like a Flatfish or Rapala, so they can be used in fly-only waters. They are extremely effective for trout during the early and late-summer streamer seasons, including fry migration time. They often, but not always, outproduce other fly patterns. Always use a loop knot for this fly so it can swim freely. Wiggle Bugs are easily tied by most tiers but are difficult to proportion and balance properly. You can contact me for an order form and for kits, tying instructions and finished Alaska flies. Larry Tullis, 5840 So. 3960 W., Taylorsville, Utah 84118. Phone 801-963-7635.

Wiggle Bugs are best fished early and late in the season, particularly the early parts of the trout season. Use a sink-tip line, 3X-0X tippet and a loop knot. Cast it down-and-across and let the current swing the fly as it swims. Picking this fly out of the water is difficult until you get the fly close because the fly wants to dive as you pull it forward. In slower water, strip the fly with long, slow strips. Set the hook when you get a firm take. You must be able to re-balance the fly after it gets chewed up so it continues to swim properly.

Woolhead Sculpins should be carried whenever fishing for bigger-than-average rainbows or char. Brown, black, olive and tan are the best colors.

Woolly Buggers work everywhere I've fished in the world and for almost every species. The common pattern calls for a marabou tail, chenille body and palmered saddle hackle. There are thousands of variations. Try flash in the tail, a crystal chenille body, lead eyes, brushed-out dubbing for the body, a different color head or a Muddler style head. A favorite variation of mine I call a Woolly Rabb-eye uses a rabbit strip and Krystal Flash for the tail, has a crystal chenille body, hackle and either a lead-eye or a Muddler head (with weighted body). Weighted bodies are important on many streamers to help them sink and to obtain a vertical as well as horizontal presentation.

Zonkers have taken many species of fish worldwide and Alaska rainbows are no exception. They have a shaped,

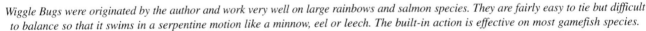

Wiggle Bugs were originated by the author and work very well on large rainbows and salmon species. They are fairly easy to tie but difficult to balance so that it swims in a serpentine motion like a minnow, eel or leech. The built-in action is effective on most gamefish species.

Dry Flies. Top Row, left to right: Black Gnat, Stimulator, Parachute Adams, Double Ugly. Middle Row: Humpy, Bullet-head Brown Stone, Thorax Dun, Renegade. Bottom Row: Gray Wulff, Bullet-head Yellow Sally, Elk Hair Caddis, California Trudel.

tube Mylar body and a rabbit strip wing. They can also be tied with the hook inverted (Byford Zonker). By varying the wing and belly color, one can imitate various minnows, leeches, lampreys, flesh and crayfish.

Dry Flies

Adams Parachute flies should be in every trout angler's box to simulate mayflies. It's a high-riding, easy-to-see and effective pattern. Anglers who have trouble seeing the white wing can substitute chartreuse or bright orange.

Black Gnats effectively imitate the various Diptera hatches commonly known as black flies. Just think of them as a fat midge.

Bullet-head Stoneflies are a great pattern for streams where stonefly hatches occur (generally in June or early July).

Double Uglys are an attractor dry fly that Jim French and I developed to imitate a cluster of insects, a stonefly adult, craneflies and cicadas (for Western states trout waters). It works in Alaska as well, not only as a dry fly but also as a streamer.

Elk Hair Caddis is the all-time best caddis dry pattern and is usually all that is needed when the caddis or small stoneflies are hatching.

Gray Wulffs have become a standard in many angler's boxes because they float well in fast water and are easily tracked. Best of all, they works.

Griffith's Gnats were created as a midge cluster and make a good gnat imitation as well. Use them when attractor patterns are rejected by picky feeders. It's difficult to track but with a small yarn strike indicator placed 18-24 inches away, you can watch the general area for a rise.

Humpies are a great suggestive pattern that will work to imitate mayflies, stoneflies, caddis and hoppers.

Renegades have long been a popular western attractor pattern and will work for uneducated fish as a dry or wet fly.

Royal Wulffs are the standard against which all other attractor dry flies are judged. If you have only one attractor dry fly in your box, it should be this one, with the Parachute Adams as a close second. It works everywhere, even to non-feeding fish or selective fish that should know better. Something about the combination of materials triggers a latent response in many fish.

Thorax Duns are good for mayflies when matching the hatch is in order.

Salmon, Pike, Grayling & Char Flies

Many of the streamer-type flies already mentioned will take species other than trout but specialized flies have been developed for each species. New flies emerge every year but I will include a list of time-tested flies in the next section on other species

V

Other Alaskan Species

SINCE MANY OF ALASKA'S FISH ARE HABITUALLY inter-related, and because you might catch several species of game fish in addition to rainbows on a given day, it is essential to know the basics about other species. Not all of Alaska's species are covered here, just those you're likely to find in or near rainbow trout waters.

Salmon are what most anglers go to Alaska to catch and if you never have, you'll want to as well, even though your main reason to visit Alaska might be huge rainbow trout.

Salmon don't really feed once they reach fresh water but there are several things that induce them to take your flies.

All game fish have a certain amount of curiosity and salmon will often sample objects around them as a means of exploring their surroundings. In nature this allows them to adapt to various conditions and changing food sources.

Lodge angler with a large male sockeye salmon.

When salmon are resting or otherwise inactive, they will seldom move much to take a fly but will intercept items that come right to their nose. This is especially true when the water is cold, low or clear. This intercept reaction will catch sockeye, chum and pink salmon when other methods fail but requires skill at putting the fly right on the salmon's nose. It's like the baseball reaction discussed earlier for trout, salmon are put in a take-it-or-pass-on-it situation and will often take the fly as it drifts right at them.

Aggravation also creates opportunities for anglers. Some lethargic trout respond to constant casts and teasing and so do salmon. Even when they are seemingly passive, the enticement of running the fly by them numerous times often gets them to strike.

Territorial behaviors can make non-feeding salmon strike the fly as well. When fish take up spawning lies, males get very territorial and will chase off or crush with their mouth anything that invades thier nest. Females aren't as aggressive but are fastidious housekeepers and will often grab a foreign object with the intent to remove it from the premises. Both instances end up with the fly in the fish's mouth and a hookup.

Sockeye (Red) Salmon

Sockeye are the most prized commercial Pacific salmon. They're excellent table fare and their fighting ability is becoming legendary despite the fact that they only became a sport fish, in angler's eyes, in the last 20-plus years. They're known as being the wildest fighter of all salmon (for their size) and are also known as being difficult and challenging to catch at times. Anglers once believed they wouldn't take flies, and even now some anglers make a skill of snagging sockeyes instead of learning how to catch them legally and properly. Sockeye do take a variety of flies and they take the most skill to catch consistently of all the Pacific salmons.

Red salmon get their name from the deep-red coloration they get when in spawning colors but they are bright silver when they enter fresh water. Starting in late June to early July, sockeyes invade most of the trophy trout waters and become, in a very integral sense, responsible for the size and quality of Alaska's trophy trout. They spawn mostly in late July through mid-September, after turning red. Some rivers have two distinct runs.

Trout eat the nymphs kicked up by nest-building sockeyes, they feed very heavily on the eggs when sockeye begin spawning, they feed on the dead salmon flesh when the egg feast is nearly finished and they feed on the newly hatched salmon alevin, fry and smolts when available. Besides that, most of Alaska's streams are fairly sterile and if it weren't for the salmon dying and adding nutrients to the streambed, there would be little or no insect base for the salmon fry and the trout to feed on. Of course the bears, eagles and other critters also eat their share, adding to the terrestrial biomass. Dead salmon bodies make it possible for the next generation to live. That's why it's not a waste for Pacific salmon to die when they're done spawning. It's all part of nature's grand design.

Sockeye salmon flies. Top Row, left to right:
Sockeye Orange, Comet, Shad Fly. Bottom Row: Sockeye Mohair, Crystal Egg, Gold Ribbed Hare's Ear.

Sockeye are known as tackle-busters and have broken countless rods and burned up numerous reels with their screaming runs and crazy, unpredictable antics. Although they can be taken on 5- or 6-weight rods, don't unless you have lots of rods to break. Seven- to 8-weights are more suitable. Floating lines and 9-foot leaders tapered to 2X, 1X or 0X are appropriate. Sink-tip lines are used for swinging-fly techniques. Flies for sockeye are smaller than most (sizes 8 to 14, heavy wire, sparsely tied) but come in a great variety and include Glo Bugs, Flash Eggs, Hare's Ear Nymphs, The Daphnia Cluster Fly, Sockeye Johns, Shad Fly, Flash Fly, Sockeye Orange and occasionally but rarely a dry fly like an Adams. Every year some new patterns become popular.

Because sockeye feed on plankton in the ocean, they are not of a predatory nature and seldom chase and seize flies. More often, you must drift or swing the fly right at nose level. They will seldom move up or down to take a fly and move very little side to side. Perhaps only 5 to 25 percent of the fish in a group will ever bite. Considering a hole might contain 50 to several thousand fish, the percentages aren't bad. The fish at the head of a resting hole, getting ready to migrate upstream, are often the most aggressive eaters.

The traditional sockeye technique drifts the fly down to the right level and then swings it right by the fish's face, at nose level. Since any one hole might have hundreds of fish in it, this method generally snags as many salmon on their backs or fins as it catches in the mouth. Even mouth-caught fish are often accidents as the leader drifts into the mouth of a non-eating salmon. The fish just mouth the fly very briefly and you must have a tight line and quick reflexes. Sockeyes are not very spooky and a 15- to 40-foot presentation to the fish is fine.

The method I prefer is a natural drift technique where a strike indicator is set up to suspend the weighted fly at the level of the fish and the fly naturally drifted without any swing or drag at all through the school of salmon. Gaudy single-egg patterns, dark-colored nymphs and sparsely tied, small salmon/steelhead patterns size 14 to 8 are my preferences for sockeye. The salmon usually mouth the fly, like they are crushing it lightly, and then release it. Very quick reactions are necessary to set the hook. The strike indicator seldom does more than bob lightly when a fish crushes the fly. The hook should be kept very sharp. Even the least amount of drag on the fly seems to turn many fish off. Lots of slack and occasional mending is necessary with this technique.

To determine if the fish are taking the fly voluntarily, see if the fly is hooked on the inside of it's mouth or if it's on the outside. The better you get at this technique, the more legally hooked sockeye you'll get but everyone will occasionally snag fish, which, legally, must be immediately released or broken off. Once you're hooked up, watch out, these fish go crazy!

King (Chinook) Salmon

These are the largest of all salmon and are highly sought after by trophy hunters. They are commonly 15 to 50 pounds and sometimes approach 100 pounds. Although there is a dedicated fly-rod following for kings, they are often ignored by anglers who prefer the more plentiful and easier-to-land species.

Kings enter rivers in May or June and then spawn through August. They are bright silver or rose colored then their colors turn darker but seldom as bright as sockeye colors but still spectacular.

Nine- to 11-weight rods are usually required to turn fish of this size as are heavy leaders of 12- to 20-pound test. You should be able to cast distances of 50 or more feet to fish the large, swift rivers that kings often (but not always) prefer. Large gaudy flies in fluorescent or dark colors are used in sizes 6 to 4/0. Patterns include the Babine Special, Double-Egg Sperm Fly, Egg Sucking Leech, The Boss, Magnum Wiggle Bug, Popsicle, Flash Fly and Coho Fly.

Steve Probasco with a nice
fly-caught king salmon from the Ayakulik River.
Kings require heavier than normal Alaska salmon tackle.

King salmon flies. Top Row, left to right: Popsicle, Flash Fly, Flash Roe. Bottom Row: Wiggle Bug, Babine Special, Boss.

Right: Silver salmon are often caught in the same watersheds as trophy Alaska rainbows.

Kings are seldom surface oriented so you must get down to their level. Sink-tip and sink-head lines are preferred, and a slow swing in front of the fish, with the fly presented broadside to the fish. If you're not catching fish, your fly is probably above or below the salmon, not at nose or eye level.

Another technique involves getting almost straight upstream from a fish and teasing the fly back and forth in front of the fish. They soon get irritated and hit the fly.

Playing large kings in big rivers is a chore. Fishing from a boat with a guide at the helm is preferred so he may maneuver the boat while you play the fish. If you're on shore, you must maneuver the fish into the slow water or probably won't land the bigger ones. All they need to do is get broadside to the current and they can run all your line out. On one particular float trip on the Chilikadrotna River, I hooked some large kings on an 8 weight and had to throw rocks opposite the fish to get them moving towards me. Most over 25 pounds just cleaned me out, the 8-weight rod and 14-pound tippet couldn't even turn them.

Silver (Coho) Salmon

By many fly-rodders, silvers are considered to be the most fun of the Pacific salmon to catch and are on a par with fresh sockeye and chums for powerful, wild antics when hooked. They take the fly aggressively, give you a great fight, jump often and also taste great on the grill. The runs

Silver salmon flies. Top Row, left to right: Flash Fly, Pink Polly, Purple Egg Sucking Leech.
Bottom Row: Wiggle Bug, Fuchsia Egg Sucking Bunny Bug, Alaskan Smolt.

peak in late July and August and provide good fishing into October or later on some waters.

They enter the rivers bright silver and when spawning turn a dark slate or dark rose color. As fresh fish migrate upstream, they will stop along current edges and in slack water areas near the main current. These areas often have large numbers of fish and provide great angling. Tidewater holes and the first holes just above tidewater are often good on many streams. Most silvers are in the 6- to 15-pound range with trophies going well over 20 pounds.

Silvers are sometimes mistaken for small king salmon because they both have spots on their backs. Remember that silvers have pinkish mouths and kings have blackish mouths.

The classic fly swing works well when there is some current and in slack water, a moderately fast retrieve is often the ticket. The fish generally hit hard and there is no doubt as to when to set the hook. Be ready for the fish to peel off line as soon as it's hooked. Try to move the hooked fish away from the school (if you can) so they don't get

Chum salmon flies. Left Column, top to bottom:
Purple Egg Sucking Leech, Fuchsia Bunny Bug. Right Column: Chartreuse Bunny Bug, Pixie Revenge.

spooked. When the fish are there but don't want to chase the flies, present smaller flies slower and drift them right at nose level with just a little swing action. I've seen times when a vertical presentation was best. We would just let a weighted fly sink in front of cruising fish and they would take the fly on the way down, as if intercepting a descending shrimp or minnow.

Silvers are more willing than most salmon to rise to the fly and will, at times, take large dry flies skittered across the surface. The Pink Pollywog, Madame X, Muddler and sometimes even mice will work when greased up and fished on an active retrieve. It's heart-stopping to watch these large fish smash the surface on the take.

Typical silver patterns include the Popsicle, Egg Sucking Leech, Wiggle Bug, Flash Fly, Coho Fly, Bunny Bugs and the dry flies previously mentioned.

Although a 6-weight rod can land many silvers, 7- or 8-weights are recommended. Use floating lines and 10-foot leaders in shallow water and fast-sink, sinking-tip lines with short, stout leaders in moderate to deep water.

Chum (Dog) Salmon

Chum salmon are called dog salmon by native Alaskans who often feed them to their sled dogs because they have less table value than sockeye, silvers or kings. This stigma has kept them as the most underrated of the salmon species. They take flies very well and are one of the finest fly-rod fish available, fighting much like the venerable Atlantic salmon, perhaps wilder.

Like all salmon in salt water, they start out a bright silver. Just before or after they enter fresh water to spawn, they start changing into their spawning colors which are mottled olives and purples, making them a startling sight when photographed or mounted. As always, the fresh, bright silver ones are most prized but all

Chum salmon fresh from the ocean are often bright silver and are very aggressive to the fly. Because they deteroriate quickly once in fresh water, they are often not targeted.

Male pink salmon showing its spawning colors and grotesque shape.

fight well until spawning and some chums get over 20 pounds.

Chums require at least a 7-weight rod and 8- or 9-weights are more common choices. Floating or sink-tip lines work well. They take flies that are swung or retrieved in front of them. Flies like Egg Sucking Leeches, Teeny Nymphs, Woolly Worms and Bunny Bugs work well. Pink or chartreuse are favorite colors.

Most enter the rivers in July and some are still present through August. The runs get better as you go north, particularly from Bristol Bay north.

Pink (Humpback) Salmon

These are possibly the most maligned of all salmon because of their relatively smaller size, poor table quality and overly abundant numbers on even-numbered years. Yet they

Pink salmon flies. Top row left to right: Babine Special, Woolly Worm, Purple Egg Sucking Bunny Bug. Bottom Row: Sockeye Orange, Polar Shrimp, Flash Fly.

Char flies. Top Row, left to right: White Egg Sucking Bunny Matuka, Black Egg Sucking Bunny Bug. Middle Row: Zonker, Purple Egg Sucking Leech. Bottom Row: Wiggle Bug, Sparkle Shrimp, Egg Fly.

Right: Angler with a nice char that was feeding on eggs.

remain a very fun fish to catch when you use tackle to match their size. They are often left alone on easily accessed rivers when the more popular salmon runs are overcrowded.

Since most anglers use 8-weight rods for salmon, these fish seem like they are no challenge but when caught on a 5- or 6-weight rod things change quickly. They are a great fish for teaching youngsters how to fly-fish and are great fun for anyone when other types of fishing is slow. If the run is good, you may experience the fastest fishing you've ever had.

Humpies, as they're affectionately known, enter streams in July and runs last through August. They change quickly when they enter fresh water. They start as great little silver bullets from 2 to 10 pounds and in a few days can turn into humpbacked, canine-fanged creatures from your worst nightmare. You often catch a mixed bag of both. They hit most salmon streamers well and also take drifted egg patterns. On the rare occasions when they aren't hitting well, try an Egg Sucking Leech fished like a nymph, just at nose level.

You might catch silver salmon, sockeyes, char or steelhead mixed in with the pinks. Rainbow trout seem to prefer the sockeye salmon's eggs whenever possible so don't spend much time fishing behind spawning pink salmon for trout if there are red salmon around.

Arctic Char & Dolly Varden

The beautifully colored arctic char and Dolly Varden are not true trout but are in the char family (along with bull trout,lake trout and brook trout). They are closely related to each other and both have sea-run and resident populations. Since there are few visual clues (Arctic char usually have a more deeply forked tail fin than Dollies), even biologists argue as to how closely they are related and which populations are which species or sub-species. The angler seldom cares what the chromosome count is as long as he or she is catching them. Anglers have come to call both by the generic term "char".

Char vary greatly in size, coloration and distribution. They are the main trout in some streams and a minority in others. Some stay pretty much in lakes and others are anadromous, staying mainly in the salt water until spawning time. A few stay in the rivers year-round but will retreat to a lake or the ocean when their favorite foods, salmon fry and salmon eggs, are gone.

Deep, clear, upper watershed lakes at the base of mountain ranges often have a char population if historically they had access to the sea. They are usually found near the inlets or outlets of the lakes but will go upstream or downstream to feed on salmon fry or salmon eggs when available.

In lakes, a 7- or 8-weight rod is desired to cast the big streamers they like in often windy conditions. Char feed on whitefish and sucker minnows or salmon and trout fry but will also occasionally take nymphs or dry flies. The bigger they are, the more carnivorous they get. Good flies include Zonkers, Matukas, Woolly Buggers, Bitch Creek Nymphs, Babine Specials and Egg Sucking Leeches.

Use floating lines and long leaders when char are feeding in the shallows but have an extra-fast sinking line available for when they go deep. When you find one char, there are usually more because they tend to school. Fishing can be either fast or nonexistent.

In rivers, char like the shallow gravel flats where salmon spawn and eggs are plentiful or the runs where they can pick off salmon fry easily. They'll also group up in the deeper holes. In some rivers, the smaller fish (6 to 17 inches) will often rise to insect hatches but big fish seldom rise, except for an occasional mouse.

The bigger fish are usually caught with streamers or using the same egg-fishing techniques described in the rainbow trout section. Char generally don't get as selective as rainbows and will often take, big, gaudy, brightly colored egg and salmon streamer patterns. Although rainbows and char are sometimes caught together, one or the other is usually dominant in a particular stream or section of stream.

Lake (Mackinaw) Trout

Lake trout are found in many lakes in Alaska north of the Kenai Peninsula and are also occasionally caught in rivers (generally these that are near lakes). Although seldom targeted by Alaska anglers, they can provide some good sporting variety and occasionally reach 20-30 pounds.

Lake trout are most often caught at inlets or outlets of lakes but will also cruise along the deep edges of weed beds and rocky reefs and drop-offs. They typically run 1 to 8 pounds but much larger ones aren't rare.

Since they are piscavores, streamers of various descriptions are used: Zonkers, Woolly Buggers, Bucktails, Egg Sucking Leeches, Wiggle Bugs and Lefty's Deceivers work well. Lake trout are often found in inlet or outlet areas where there is just the smallest amount of current, especially in early summer when the salmon smolts are migrating and again in the early fall when they group up to spawn.

Lodge client with a surprise lake trout from a river below a lake.

Lake trout flies. Left Column, top to bottom: White Bunny Bug, Chartreuse Bunny Matuka, Black Bunny Matuka.
Right Column: Lefty's Deceiver, Purple Egg Sucking Leech, Wiggle Bug.

Individuals also may be caught in river areas, long distances from any lake, but these are inconsistent and are probably migrating fish. The salmon fry and smolts are their preferred food choice but lake trout will eat most any other fish from one inch to 16 inches long.

Fish sinking-tip lines or full-sinking lines from a boat and use imitations of their foods or attractor streamers. Fish for them as you would fish streamers for trout. Cast out and across, let the fly sink close to the bottom and do some long strips with pauses. Fighting lakers is a tug of war. They seldom jump or run long distances but especially in rivers can fight very well.

Arctic Grayling

These pretty fighters are highly prized by some anglers because in Alaska they can reach trophy sizes of 4, 5 or more pounds. Their iridescent colors, exotic fins and tendency to feed on dry flies make them a very desirable addition to the angler's catch. They get large the same way the trout do, by eating salmon fry and eggs. They will also eat almost anything they can fit into their small mouths and are sometimes caught by surprised trout fishermen. Anytime there is a gnat, midge, mayfly or caddis hatch, the grayling will feed on the surface, giving fly anglers a nice variation to the egg or streamer fishing.

Each stream has a certain biomass that it can support and grayling often inhabit different areas from trout. Grayling like the deeper rocky pools below rapids, the outside current edges of cut banks and gravel tailouts. At some times of the year, especially in June, there is often a nice mix of trout and grayling that will take dry flies and small nymphs. The rest of the year, grayling will often school up in areas where few trout are, when trout usually feed in the salmon spawning gravel runs where eggs and nymphs are plentiful. Some side streams are full of grayling when the main rivers have only a few. Small char and grayling are often found mixed together.

Floating lines, 9-foot tapered leaders and 3X or 4X tippet are the norm. They are seldom leader shy and only drag

Arctic grayling are great on a dry fly, nymph or streamer and are one of Alaska's magical draws.

conscious in heavily fished areas. It's not uncommon to catch 30, 50, 100 or even more in a day when conditions are right.

Since grayling have smallish mouths, most anglers use dry flies, nymphs, eggs and streamers in hook sizes 16 to 10. Fly patterns include, Black Gnats, Elk Hair Caddis, Adams, Trudes, Royal Wulffs, Rubber Leg Nymphs, Gold Ribbed Hare's Ears, Prince Nymphs, Fry Flies and Egg Flies.

Northern Pike

Northern pike are the barracudas of fresh water. They are very effective predators and live in the sloughs and side lakes of many Alaskan rivers. Pike are plentiful in certain latitudes of the Northern Hemisphere in North America, Europe and Russia and are highly underrated as a game fish. Their long, lean bodies can generate short bursts of incredible speed. When their feeding habits are surface oriented, pike can create heart-stopping boils that look like a bowling ball was thrown into the lake. Those that

experience pike fishing often become devotees. Pike average 2 to 12 pounds in Alaska and can reach 20 to 30-plus pounds.

Specific tackle and flies are a must. Eight- to 10-weight rods are typical to cast the big flies that are required to interest pike. Their rows of teeth are sharp enough to cut through 20-pound-test monofilament leader so a thin wire bite tippet of 9 to 12 inches is necessary on the end of a short, heavy, tapered leader. Although floating lines are often adequate, by late summer the fish might be deep enough to require a fast-sinking line. Since their surface strikes are so spectacular, many stick with surface poppers or surface streamers unless they fail to bring the fish up.

Pike flies vary from long rabbit-strip leeches and long-tailed streamers to poppers and divers. Big is the key here. Pike seldom take flies under 3 inches long and some go 12 inches long. Large Lefty's Deceivers, Dahlberg's MegaDivers, Sea-Ducers, Long Rabbit Zonkers, Magnum Woolly Buggers, saltwater poppers and Magnum Wiggle

Grayling flies. Top Row, left to right: Thunder Creek Special, Prince Nymph, Royal Wulff. Bottom Row: Egg Fly, Hare's Ear, Adams.

Pike flies. Left Column, top to bottom: Sea-Ducer, Flute Fly, Popper. Right Column: Bucktail Wiggle Bug, Bend Back, Bunny.

Bugs are all effective in hook sizes 1 to 3/0. Many are tied with weed guards because of the weedy and snag-filled waters that pike prefer.

Although trout and pike seldom inhabit the same areas, they can often be found closeby. Look for dark, weedy lakes or sloughs that are connected to a slow, meandering river or lakes of low elevation. Pike prefer shallow, dark-bottomed bays in early summer and the deeper edges of weed beds and rocky shelves as the water warms.

Pike like to follow flies right up to the boat so polarized fishing glasses are a must. If one follows but doesn't take, the angler can often jig the fly or make figure-8 movements with the rod to induce the fish to take,. They often thrash at the fly just as it reaches the surface. If you miss a strike, immediately slap the fly back into the water, because pike are apt to hit again.

Retrieves are basic. Either a slow jigging retrieve or a medium-fast strip are generally adequate. Poppers are popped loudly at first, to get the pike's attention, and then popped steadily across the surface. Don't set the hook until the fish turns, unless it swims straight at you. Set the hook swiftly and with power. Pike are often played to the boat or shore only to have the fish open up its mouth and spit the fly back at you, having never actually been hooked.

The author with a 17-pound pike from the Iliamna area. With all the other good fishing in the area, pike often get overlooked.

VI
Russian Rainbows

SINCE THE EARLY 90S, FAR EASTERN RUSSIA HAS been opening up to Western anglers. The Kamchatka Peninsula is the part of Russia you'll hit if you follow the Aleutian Island chain westward from Alaska, or if you look north of Japan. It offers incredible opportunities on almost untouched rainbow, steelhead, char and salmon waters to those who have a sense of adventure and the capital that is needed to travel there. For those who seek adventure and want to see a place that is still like Alaska was 50-plus years ago, there's no better place. Due to its close geographic location to the United States, this area once held many sensitive military installations. Even native Russians were restricted from many areas here. It has remained largely pristine and some waters are virtually untouched by humans. Imagine fishing areas where no one has ever sport-fished before. These places are available in abundance in far eastern Russia.

I actually delayed the writing of this book until I was able to go there myself so I could add a chapter from first-hand experience. It was one of the most memorable adventures I've ever experienced and recommend it to all adventurers, as long as the political and social climate is stable. Trips are available from several sources. I chose those sponsored by the Wild Salmon Center.

We flew from Seattle (the Wild Salmon Center's headquarters) to Anchorage and from Anchorage to Petropovlovsk on Alaska Airlines (about a 4-hour flight). I personally hope another airline will do the trip soon because we got very poor service from Alaska Airlines, regarding baggage, some of which didn't make it even though we were charged extra for being a little overweight on baggage. From Petropovlovsk we were transported by bus 7 1/2 hours north to the frontier town of Esso, a sleepy little village with interesting geothermal features and incredible vegetable gardens. Our outfitter maintains a small apartment there where gear for the trip is stored. All you need to bring is your personal sleeping gear, clothing and fishing gear. Food,

On the Sedanka River, more than half of a trout's summer diet is mice.

tents, rafts, utensils and so forth were provided. We loaded up one of the large military-style helicopters and flew 1 1/2 hours over some incredible wilderness to our destination watershed.

Our group floated the Sedanka River, a tributary of the Tigil on the western side of the Kamchatka Peninsula. It's a moderately-paced river that we floated in inflatable rafts and kick-boats, setting up camp for several days between floats. There was one jet motor on a Zodiac-style raft for mobility. It would be difficult to imagine better fishing. It was easy to catch 50 to over 120 rainbows, kundzha (Siberian white-spotted char), Dolly Varden and silver salmon a day on mice patterns, streamers and dry flies. The trout averaged 2-4 pounds and went up to 6 pounds and 5-14 pounds for the silver salmon.

The Russian staff was very competent but don't expect them to guide you like an American lodge might. They cooked traditional Russian dishes, sang folk songs and even hunted for fresh food. They were very good at moving us through the paperwork in town and took good care of us on the road and in the backcountry.

Our exploratory trip was oriented towards resident trout species. Other rivers on the Kanchatka Peninsula have larger but fewer resident trout. Some friends floated the Zhupanova River, lower on the peninsula, and got into some 20- to 30-inch trout but much fewer of them, averaging 6-12 a day per person.

Other trips the Wild Salmon Center sponsors are fall trips for Kamchatka steelhead, that grow to 30 pounds. I'm not completely familiar with the steelhead camps but I gather that they are mostly medium and small watersheds that are fished near the estuaries from semi-permanent camps, with jet boats as transportation. I've heard numbers from one fish a week to 6 or more steelhead a day.

The resident rainbows we caught on the Sedanka River were thought, by the scientists, to be a very old form. This rainbow has cutthroat slashes under its jaw and full redband coloration but it is not a hybrid between the two species, more likely it's an older form, possibly from before the two split ways biologically. They fought well and were extremely fun on topwater mouse techniques. Mice were especially effective on the smaller side channels but the fish would take mice patterns anywhere as long as they were slowly twitched across the surface by keeping the rod high and bouncing the tip. The scientists told us that 60% of the trout's diet was mice. All the streamer patterns we had worked very well also, and included Zonkers, Matukas, Woolly Buggers and Wiggle Bugs. Morning and evening brown mayfly hatches brought up many of the fish under 18 inches on Adams and Wulffs.

No float planes here.

Beautiful Siberian char.

The Dolly Varden or arctic char we caught were both resident and sea-run and surprised me by taking mice patterns and jumping occasionally. The same methods that took rainbows also took char but they seemed to hole up in slightly slower water than the rainbows.

The kundzha is a Russian char that has typical char background coloration but with big white spots covering the body. They were great fighters that took dry flies, streamers and mice patterns. Dry flies for the smaller ones and meat for the larger ones. We caught none over 6 pounds but I've heard of other rivers where they get so large you needed a 10-weight fly-rod for them. Don't confuse these with the inland Siberian taimen which can attain incredible sizes to 100-plus pounds. No rivers in Kamchatka, that I'm aware of, have the taimen.

The Kamchatka silvers we caught looked, fought and took flies the same as Alaskan silvers. They mostly occurred down near the confluence of the Tigil and in the Tigil itself. Pinks, sockeye and chums were all present in small numbers but most were close to death and so were not good sportfish in our time period of late August to mid-September.

While there we also saw eagles, brown bears, carabou, ducks and sables. There are supposedly 30,000 brown bear in Kamchatka and they do get hunted regularly by locals and by Americans. The two bears I saw ran away fast when they saw us nearby.

The Wild Salmon Center, the organizer of my trip, is a non-profit organization that takes American anglers into the backcountry. They have a 20-year agreement with the Russian government to bring in sponsors that will help fund scientific research in the unstudied areas of Kamchatka. Trying to go on your own would probably be fruitless. You need contacts and experienced outfitters to get you through the excessive bureaucracy smoothly. The traveling anglers help pick up the tab for scientists from both countries (a 1997 sponsorship costs $5000-$6500 for 2 weeks, plus airfare to Petropovlovsk and incidentals, plan on about $8000 total). Much of the sponsorship cost for the trip is for the helicopter transportation, which is very pricey. Anglers collect biological samples for the Russian and American scientists and the scientists do what they do. Since you are helping an official multi-country

Russian silver salmon

The char species of Kamchatka eat mice just like their Alaskan counterparts.

cooperative scientific expedition, the entire trip is tax deductable.

The studies are designed to help develop sustainable sport and commercial fisheries and make recommendations for future economical development (guides, lodges, outfitters, tourism, etc.) in this financially depressed region. The biological data collected will also go a long way towards understanding the Pacific fisheries and how they interrelate. This research should prove to be very valuable in developing fisheries from the ground up instead of being reactionary like so many of the fisheries elsewhere. There are commercial fisheries operating around Russia that

caught on a Wiggle Bug.

harvest salmon in the ocean but steelhead and other forms of rainbow of Kamchatka have been protected from commercial harvest since 1983.

Since you, as a sponsor, are aiding in opening up new untried waters, sometimes the fishing might be less than perfect. It has happened with some of the groups. This is one of those deals where you pay your money and take your chances. For me the chance was worth it because how often do you get to fish unfished, wilderness waters. As studies progress, the best fisheries will become apparent and further studies on those watersheds will permit more predictable fishing.

There are several other commercial operations providing rafting, sightseeing and angling opportunities. The most well-known fishing operation is Tony Sarp's Katmai Lodge, which has had many successful rainbow and kundzha trout trips to a lodge on the Zhupanova River near Petropovlovsk, where trout to 30-plus inches have been caught, photographed and released. Check the Internet for others.

Kamchatka is primed for a burst of tourism but most of its residents have not discovered how to welcome and exploit American travelers yet. Unfortunately, there is still an amount of suspicion and prejudice concerning Americans, a holdover from the Cold War, but the younger generations are enjoying their newfound freedoms, even if old ways die hard. The KGB replacement, I'm not sure what they call themselves now, hassled us a little on the way home but ended up being very polite, and even acted as tour guides in Petropovlovsk. It goes with saying that we need to be friendly and on our best behavior so they have no reason to close the borders to American anglers.

VII

Alaskan Wildlife

YOU'RE LIKELY TO SEE MANY CRITTERS IN Alaska, other than fish. Alaska is blessed with an abundance of wildlife and no trip there is complete without seeing some of it. Learning something about the animals before you go helps you mentally prepare for the trip. Here are some of my observations and suggestions about dealing with the wildlife. Your views and other experienced travelers may differ. Your job is to learn all you can from various sources and form a philosophy of interaction for yourself. The best advice I can give about animals is to keep far enough away from them so you don't disturb their normal activities. As any wilderness traveler knows, however, that isn't possible all the time.

Bears

Part of the Alaska experience is seeing bears. It's an exciting part of the trip. Horror stories about bear attacks abound but are mostly untrue, fictionalized accounts conjured up by those seeking to be more macho or just to embellish their stories. Bear attacks are rare and generally misrepresented when they do happen. Usually it's just a bear that wanders into camp and people assume that it's after them. Maybe it's a mother bear growling at or false charging you to let you know she won't stand for you messing with her cubs. Bear charges are rare and 99% are false charges. Close encounters can end badly for the bears even though it's extremely rare for a bear to actually touch someone. I've been within 100 yards of over 1000 grizzly or brown bears (that I saw, many more that I didn't see) in my fishing and camping adventures in Alaska and Russia and have never felt my life was in imminent danger.

Bears are going to be in the areas you fish, using the same resources, so get used to the idea. They don't look on us as competitors but rather as a super-predator. Most bears

Bears and rainbows both owe their bulk to salmon.

have learned a certain respect for humans and keep a respectable distance. Yet there's something about human conceit that makes us fear bears because they are bigger, faster, stronger and conceivably, can eat us. We don't like being second in the food chain, so in most areas of the southern 48 we've made ourselves more comfortable by killing off the things we fear.

In Alaska, some bears are killed each year because of fear or as hunting trophies but there are many bears that are not hunted and that use the same fisheries we do and get used to our presence just as we get used to theirs. Generally, there is a healthy respect between the two. Most of the trophy rainbow fisheries in Alaska are that way and bears are part of what Alaska is all about. Let's go through some of my basic suggestions for dealing with the presence of bears and you can decide for yourself.

Most of the bears in our rainbow trout waters are coastal grizzly, usually called brown bears. Some areas have black bears but they are seen less in southwestern Alaska because the bigger brown bears often kill them. Brown bears are more predictable than black bears. Stay out of their way, don't surprise them at close range and keep smelly foods and other scented items out of camp and they generally won't bother you. Try to keep at least 150 feet from any bear. Bears have fairly poor distance eyesight but have excellent hearing and sense of smell. It's not uncommon for a bear to wander towards you or vice versa. Bears spend most of their time walking around looking for salmon, berries, roots or rodents to eat or are resting somewhere.

When traveling on foot, you must take action or risk getting too close to a bear. If you're moving, keep talking, whistling, ringing a small bell or singing to warn bears of your approach. A resting bear will usually move out of your

A large bear wandering the windy shoreline of Kukaklek Lake.

way. Surprising a sleeping bear at close range is a real bad idea because it has two choices, attack or flee. I prefer the better, long-distance odds.

If you're floating a river and see a bear downstream, alert the bear if he has not seen you by yelling. Pull over to the far side of the river, well above him, and if he seems unaggressive, pass by with the current.

When you see a bear, don't panic. First, call to the bear and wave your hat to let it know you're there if it hasn't seen or heard you yet. Alert the other members of your party about the bear. Often, the bear will take off away from you on its own. If it continues towards you, it's your responsibility to get yourself away from the bear. Do this by walking away about 90 degrees from its approach. Wade across to the other side of the stream or back up away from the river or trail to let the bear pass. This is his home and you should let him have right of way. Never run away from a bear because it may trigger the chase instinct in even a non-aggressive bear.

Occasionally a bear will be aggressive towards you anyway and keep walking towards you even when you try to move out of its way. These are usually young males testing their domain, seeing what they can get away with. It may be a bear that has learned that humans usually have food near them. They are very curious and in the past may have raided coolers or packs left unattended and found food. They may even have learned that spooked people will drop their packs and run, leaving a Scooby-snack for them. Don't drop your pack and run. You can't teach bears that it's okay to push you around or they will continue to do it to yourself and others and someone will eventually shoot the problem bear or the bear may harm a human.

These mildly aggressive bears can generally be chased off in a couple of ways. It doesn't take much to spook a bear that was previously aggressive. I've found the best way to get one of these bears to leave the area is to throw rocks. Some "experts" say not to throw rocks but I've always had semi-aggressive brown bears back off after a few rocks and I've thrown them at about 5 dozen different brown bears.

Now remember, you should not let a bear get that close in the first place but if one won't leave you alone, try throwing rocks 1/2 fist size or smaller. Bears seldom see the rock until it's close and when the rock hits them or the ground or water beside them, they are often startled. They don't relate you to the rock and get spooked. Several rocks in succession usually gets the bear nervous enough to leave. Don't throw rocks at a sow with cubs. Never try to hit a bear with a stick or your rod. It will relate that to you and might get more aggressive.

The other way to chase a bear off is with a noise-maker. Many backcountry anglers and guides carry firearms for

A ground squirrel that has no fear of man but squeaks like crazy when a bear approaches. A great bear alarm.

their own and their clients' peace of mind. A gun being fired off in the air, only occasionally frightens a bear. Most bears have not learned to link up the sound of a gun with danger. For the ones that have, it's usually too late.

Some anglers carry noisy boomers or firecracker loads that can be shot out of a shotgun or special starter-type pistol. It's like a firecracker being shot near or at the bear and the concussion and sound near the bear spook it. These are generally available at sporting goods stores in Alaska. If rocks don't keep a bear out of camp, these sometimes do the trick. Just make sure you don't make the round explode on the opposite side of the bear because it will run away from the concussion, towards you. If the bear is close, bounce the noise-maker round off the ground between you and the bear.

Bear protection in the form of firearms is optional and there are philosophical differences. Many anglers and guides carry firearms for the peace of mind that, if the rare did happen, you'd have one more recourse for self-protection. Others don't like firearms and the responsibility they bring. Both options are okay but if you carry one, and use it in anything but the most life-threatening of situations, you will have to answer to the authorities.

Appropriate firearm protection includes 12-gauge shotguns loaded with buckshot and slugs and .44 Mag or bigger handguns. A gun not carried on your person is a useless gun so it's best to have a police-style (short barrel/short stock) pump shotgun with a sling or a pistol in a handy holster, in other words, easy access, close-range weapons.

Carrying guns to Alaska is easy as long as you're not trying to get them from one country to another. Keep them in a locked case in one check-on bag and the ammo in another. You are required to declare guns at the check-in desk. Don't try to carry-on any part of the firearms or ammo on your person.

Pepper spray has been hyped to work on bears but the results are unpredictable at best. First of all, commercial airlines won't allow you to carry the canisters on-board. Even float-plane pilots won't let the things inside the plane. If one ever punctured inside the plane you can imagine the problems. A canister sealed in an ammo can might be allowed in a float-planes' pontoon lockers. One guide I talked to sprayed a bear at 10 feet and it just shook its head, the spray had little or no effect. Another Alaska floatplane pilot I know peppered a bear at close range with no results. Everyone I know that promotes pepper spray over firearms have never actually used it on a brown bear. If you have an actual pepper spray experience, I'd like to hear about it. Another problem with sprays is that Alaska's winds are not always in your favor and the pepper spray might be blown back at you. Bears also like strong smells and are attracted to items sprayed with pepper spray so never spray your gear or tent thinking that will repel bears. It's only hope of working is to spray it directly into the bear's eyes and nose to disorient it long enough for you to escape.

Bears learn very quickly and have an intelligence somewhere above that of a dog and can be trained. Unfortunately, some of the training it gets is to relate the sound of a noisy fly or spinning reel to fish. Certain bears will go toward the sound of a noisy reel and take the salmon right off your line. It's an easy meal for them and quite a shock for the angler. It's never happened to me. This has mainly been reported in coastal areas where fresh salmon are abundant and seldom occurs on rainbow trout waters. Don't try to stop the bear or fight it for the fish. Instead, use a quiet reel or move to another area, away from this bear's territory.

Camping in bear country is a fine art. Some anglers don't have the nerve to do it, but for others, it can be an exhilarating adventure. The biggest bears often are shy and come out only at night, after the fly-in anglers leave for the lodge. There are several ways to keep yourself from having bear problems in camp.

Put your tent up in an area that is out of the way of normal bear routes. Just assume the banks and back channels belong to the bears, also any other areas where bear trails are visible. Camping 200 feet or more from a waterway is a good idea and is the rule on some waters. On private lands, river-access laws generally state that you can navigate the river as long as you stay within the high-water mark, this includes camping. You must camp on a gravel bar or an island to be within federal navigable waterway laws. Here again, pick a spot that isn't littered with salmon carcasses and that is away from bear trails or bear beds (bear-sized flattened vegetation). Area ownership and management can be found by looking at the information in an Alaska floating guide-book or from the authorities.

Cook, eat and clean fish 100 yards or more or from camp so that any food scraps spilled won't attract curious bears into your camp. Food choices are important so you don't have smelly, fresh foods sitting around to attract bears. I prefer to take dried foods, individually sealed in plastic or foil pouches. I then double bag the food in sealed trash bags to prevent any smells from permeating the area and stash it 100 yards from camp. Never store or eat foods in the tent. Dehydrated, dried or freeze-dried food isn't that tasty but it's better than bear problems. You may also want to keep clothing that may contain cooking odors in sealed bags 100 yards from camp.

A storage option is a bear-resistant canister. They are available from some outdoor sports retailers or can be borrowed from the Forest Service, who provide them for backcountry campers. Hanging the food in a tree, away from camp is not always an option because most areas don't have trees or they are often stunted in growth. Keep a

A misplaced food bag ended up as bear munchies.

clean camp and you'll have few, if any, problems. If a bear does get your food, you'll have to eat fish, berries and maybe ptarmigan the rest of the trip (things could be worse). If you do eat salmon or grayling, cook them away from camp or eat fish for lunch so you can just float or walk away from the remains.

If you camp in bear country, you will have bears in camp at night. They are naturally curious creatures and I've had trips where bears sniffed through camp every night. The experience of having a bear so close to your tent wall is intense. Some people can't handle it. Any sound outside becomes magnified 100 times and you just know that every rustle of the bushes or salmon flopping in the stream is a bear walking by.

I've experienced a number of sleepless hours myself, straining to hear real or imagined sounds outside, until I learned a trick—ear plugs! They work well to deaden the overtaxed sense of hearing that prevents sleep and also are great if your buddies snore too loud. I figure that if a bear is going to get me, he'll have to wake me up first. I'm not going to lose sleep over imagined dangers. I do, however, keep my firearm handy, also a flashlight, a knife to cut my way out of the back of the tent if I need to and some easy-on shoes and coat. Precautions I've never used, and hope to never use.

The only real problem I ever had with bears in camp was when I improperly stashed my bag of snacks in some bushes just 25 feet from my tent. I was rudely awakened by two bears growling and fighting over the spoils, just a few feet outside my tent.

Just remember that bears are ruled by their belly and that you need to stash food and anything else with a strong smell properly and you will likely have no problems. Scented lotions, perfumes and sexual smells have also been known to attract bears.

If the worst does happen and you are attacked, actually touched by a bear, drop down to the ground in the fetal position and clasp your hands behind your neck. If you have a pack on, it may shield you. Remain still until the bear loses interest and wanders out of sight.

Remember that if you choose to be in bear country, there are no guarantees for your safety but you can lessen the odds considerably with a little knowledge. Read all you can to prepare yourself mentally. Bears are part of the adventure. If you knew the exact outcome of every trip it wouldn't be an adventure and it would be wrong to eliminate the bears just so you could feel more comfortable, and vice versa.

Moose

Moose scare me more than bears. I've been chased by moose several times that just moments before seemed

Southwest Alaska has many trophy caribou because they put energy into growing instead of long migrations.

Caribou

Caribou are synonymous with Alaska and many fishing areas have populations nearby. It's not uncommon for one to wander near camp or see several ford the river you're fishing or floating. Caribou are skittish and generally don't stay around long. Hunters prize the racks of these southwest Alaska trophies because they put more energy into their growth, instead of migration than do their northern cousins.

I've never been bothered by caribou but some clients told me that they were once chased down a coastal beach by a large, irritated caribou. They hid in some driftwood log piles and threw flotsam at the beast until it left.

Ptarmigan are plentiful in Alaska.

docile and uninterested in my presence. They are unpredictable but great to watch, just don't get too close. If one causes problems, throw rocks at it and make loud noises to scare it away. Keep a tree or other large object between you and the problem animal.

Normally, moose are skittish and will move away from your approach because they are hunted regularly in Alaska. The biggest moose like to go into the thickest bear brush (alder thickets) and rest. They come out to graze or to challenge rival bulls. Alaskan moose are known as the biggest anywhere.

A cormorant in Bristol Bay.

Birds

There are a variety of large predatory or scavenging birds in Alaska. Bald eagles are common in many watersheds and can be seen feasting on salmon carcasses. Osprey prefer live fish and will swoop down and hit the water with their talons to snare fish. Ravens are large and efficient scavengers. Loons and other fish-eating ducks arrive early and stay until the temperatures dip. Ptarmigans and pine hens are everywhere. Many herons are around as well, feeding on salmon fry and other small fish.

Harlequins, eider ducks and many others birds use Alaska as a nesting and feeding area. Some birds fly south for the winter, including some that will fly to South America or Antarctica each year. Over 400 species of birds

Canadian geese often summer in Alaska.

have been recorded in Alaska, including tundra swans, Canadian geese, emperor geese, brant geese, snow geese, sandhill cranes, puffins, kittiwakes and many others.

Although seldom seen as a threat, nesting birds can be very protective and might dive-bomb you. Songbirds won't be much of a threat but eagles, owls or other large predatory birds might be. They have been known to slash those that get too close to nests with their razor-sharp talons. Just keep a safe distance from nesting birds. As with other wildlife, if you disturb their regular habits, you're probably too close.

Another curious Alaska explorer.

Other Critters

In your Alaskan travels, you might see many other animals. Red foxes are common and seldom fear humans unless they've been hunted. I've had them come right up to me and eat out of my hand during a lunch break. Wolverines are uncommon and very secretive. Wolves are pretty common but difficult to locate, as they are naturally shy of people. You might see a lynx or bobcat. In remote areas up north

there are musk ox but you're not going to see them near any rainbow trout waters. Alaska even has its own population of wild bison. Sitka deer, elk and some white tails are present in the south. Trout mecca Lake Iliamna has a population of freshwater seals, one of only two populations in the world. The other is Lake Baikal in Russia. Seals, walruses, whales and dolphins are all present on the coast and can sometimes be viewed in coastal areas.

Dall sheep can be seen in mountainous areas.

There really is a wealth of wildlife in Alaska and it is worth your while to make special efforts to view them when there. In other words, don't get so keyed up in the fishing that you miss Alaska's other delights. Alaska must be seen as a total experience.

This red fox had no natural fear of man and came to share our lunch.

VIII
Planning Your Alaskan Trip

Lodges, Tent Camps & Guides

PREPARATION IS THE KEY TO A SUCCESSFUL Alaskan adventure. Whether you simply call up a lodge a friend recommended or you put a full-blown expedition together, there are some preparations you should make.

If good food, good guides, good service and great fishing are your requirements, you should turn your trip over to some of the excellent lodges available in Alaska. However, you should only turn yourself over to a lodge after you've done some research.

I've had the chance to visit a number of lodges and each has its own focus and personality. For example: Rainbow River Lodge, where I guided, is a rainbow trout flyfishing lodge. We fished 95% of the time with flies and 75% of the time for rainbows. The rest of the time was divided between the salmon species, char, lake trout, steelhead, pike and grayling. The rainbow trout waters we fished were catch-and-release-only, fly-fishing-only waters and small numbers of salmon were kept in season. There were equal numbers of fly-outs and local, jet-boat trips.

Anglers who want to come back from Alaska with lots of dead salmon would be better off signing up with another lodge that specializes in salmon and that caters to meat fishermen. Another lodge on my home river was strictly a local, Ma and Pa kind of lodge, they had no fly-outs available, less expensive but also fewer options.

Some "lodges" turn out to be tent camps, some with jet-boat transportation and some without. The transportation costs and lodging quality are what make some lodges cost more than others when visiting (in Alaska). Float planes are expensive to buy, operate and maintain but they give you the best variety and options for your trip.

Lunch at a beautiful fly-out fishing hole.

66

Tent camps are less comfortable and less versatile but much lower priced. If you book yourself into a tent camp, make sure you know about the guides and jet boats. Some inexpensive tent camps are do-it-yourself affairs where they just supply transportation to and from, the food and the tents. Fishing is on your own. If you want a guide and a boat for mobility, make sure they are available. Most tent camps are located in great salmon fishing areas where trout and other species may or may not be an option. Find out which species will be available at your camp at your scheduled time of year. If your mobility is limited, you may have poor fishing in-between salmon runs. Timing is critical if you fish one area and don't have fly-out or jet-boat options.

When looking for a lodge, ask your friends about their experiences. Seek out several lodges listed in the fishing magazines you subscribe to and they will likely list the lodges that cater to your type of angler. Check them out by calling for a brochure and price list and asking any questions that concern you. Also ask for a list of references. Call all the references and ask questions that they might answer in more detail than the lodge owners. Popular

Taking the right gear is important on a do-it-yourself wilderness float.

weeks fill up fast, often one year in advance, so lodge owners naturally try to fill up their slow weeks. Ask when the best weeks are for the specific type of fishing you want. If you ask very specific questions, you will get better answers than if you just ask if the fishing is good in a particular week.

A good guide from a good lodge can make your trip for you. Unfortunately, Alaska is notorious for its selection of good and bad guides. Once you determine which lodge is for you, ask specifically for a guide that suits your needs. Here again, be specific. If you are a relative novice, ask for one that is good with beginners. If you want one that is very knowledgeable, that an advanced angler can learn from (that may or may not be patient with beginners), ask for the top guide. If you just want to relax and fish, ask for a guide that cooks a good shore lunch. If you are not too steady on your feet or can't walk far, ask the lodge owner about easy access to fishing areas and experience in dealing with handicapped anglers. Some spots require rather vigorous hikes and wading. Some lodges cater to handicapped people, others can't.

You get the picture. You're paying the money and should get what you ask for. Top lodges get $3000 to $6000 or more per week per person, airfare to closest Alaskan town not included.

Lodges are nice because you can leave many of the details and logistics up to them. All you need to do is bring your personal gear and fishing tackle. Some lodges even provide the tackle for you.

Here is a list of recommended gear for going to a lodge:
Clothing: Thin and thick socks (wool and synthetics), thermal underwear, 2 changes of fishing wear (long/short sleeve shirts, pants etc.) plus lodge and travel clothing,

Well-stocked fly-tying benches are set up at all top lodges for guests to tie hot patterns.

warm coat, hiking shoes, travel shoes. **Fishing:** Fishing hat, warm hat, 2 pair polarized sunglasses, chest waders (neoprene or breathable membrane with patch kits), wading shoes, gravel guards, fleece pants, wading rain jacket (waterproof/breathable preferred), fingerless gloves, fly rods: 6-weight and an 8-weight, plus one back-up rod, fly reels, x-spool w/floating and sink-tip fly lines, fishing vest or pack, fly boxes and flies, tapered leaders, tippets, split shot, strike indicators, fly floatant, hemostats, nippers, optional: spin rod/reel/line/lures. **Personal:** Flashlight, bathroom tissue, razor, medication, plane tickets, money, travelers checks, bank checks, shampoo, soap, toothbrush/paste, insect repellent, first-aid kit, pocketknife or knife tool, hand warmers. Optional: Camera, film, batteries, personal stereo, recordings, books, travel guides, journal, pencil, art supplies, special beverages, snacks etc.

Fly-outs

If a top-notch lodge and guide just isn't in the cards, there are several other ways to do fly-outs that include day trips, wilderness cabins or a camping option.

Anglers based out of a town might want to consider a day or two of fly-out fishing. Because of the number of float planes in Anchorage, fly-outs from there might be crowded. It's often better to fly a commuter plane to a smaller town and catch an air taxi from there to less-fished waters.

The air-taxi floatplane operators are a very valuable source of information. They are on the water in remote areas every day, year after year and they can tell you where the best salmon runs are or where you can catch trout.

Packaged day trips are often sold by air-taxi operators and might include some sightseeing as well as some fishing. Some planes will stay with you while you fish, others have other clients to pick-up and deliver and will return for you at the end of the day. You should have a day pack with emergency clothing and food for day trips because of the unpredictable nature of Alaskan weather. You might be stuck there overnight if the area gets weathered-in. Trust in the float plane pilot's ability to predict weather and don't go if he says it's poor or edgy flying weather. Always be very sure of the time and the location of the return flight. Be there.

Instead of day trips, you may want a floatplane service to fly you into a wilderness cabin for a week. Private cabins or Forest Service cabins are available in many areas where salmon fishing is good. You must bring your own food unless you buy a package deal that includes meals. Some have motorboats available for increased mobility. Find out what the cabin is equipped with, most are pretty rustic, usually without running water, comfortable bedding or electricity.

Without the Alaska bush plane, many waters would be extremely difficult to access.

Camping out yourself is another option. Here again, some outfitters will provide you with tents, food and transportation while others will simply transport you where you want to be dropped off with your gear. Strategic planning is a must and the air-taxi operators are the best source for up-to-date infomation on the best places to camp and fish. Make sure you have everything you need because you are not likely to get it at the corner convenience store. If you're there for a week and forget your sleeping bag or raingear, you might be in a dangerous survival situation. You can often pre-arrange for a float plane to come get you and transport you to a second or third location during the course of your outing. See the section on float fishing for a more complete camping guide. If you need to come out early, you can sometimes make arrangements with another pilot that is there dropping off or picking up clients. But don't bet on that except in heavily used areas.

All of these fly-out options can provide you with some good fishing that should cost less than the daily rate at a lodge. You should plan on $350 to $600 an hour for a float

Planning Your Alaskan Trip

plane (round trips). This fee is usually divided up between several anglers or they may charge each person a flat fee. A DeHaviland Beaver float plane can usually carry 6 anglers and minimal gear for a day, or 3-4 persons with camping and rafting gear. Call the air taxi operators for current rates and weight restrictions.

Float & Camp Trips

The most adventurous way to see Alaska is the float trip. Float trips are where the pilot drops you and your party off upriver and picks you up downriver. You get to see some wilderness waters that seldom see anglers and have a great camping and floating/fishing adventure. Do-it-yourself trips require extensive planning and logistics, guided floats are better for the angler that's unsure about his or her wilderness travel skills.

On a guided float, the outfitter will supply you with a list of recommended personal gear to bring. The guide generally handles a raft for you while you fish. He then sets up camp and cooks the meals for you. If you want a guide to do his best for you, help with camp chores. He generally works from 6 in the morning till 10 at night and any help you give setting up tents, cooking, washing dishes or loading the boat will mean more time for him to help you catch fish. Some require your agreement to help before the trip starts. If you're not into camp chores, don't do this trip, seek a lodge that will cater to your preferences.

When camping in Alaska, remember to treat the wilderness with respect. Much of Alaska still has intact natural environments and we have the responsibility to keep them that way.

Modern wilderness travel dictates that we adopt the philosophy of minimum impact. Any travel in pristine areas will leave some impact but we can reduce the amount to a minimum level by adopting some travel habits:
•Leave only footprints and take only photos.
•If you pack it in, pack it out.
•If someone else leaves it, you can do your part by removing it.
•Leave a place as good or better than you found it.
•Camp and latrines at least 200 feet from waterways if possible.
•Make no fires or limit fires to safe areas and extinguish them completely.
•Make fires on rocks or gravel bars, not on the tundra.
•Don't cut live trees, use driftwood for fires.

These travel habits will make you a better, more conscientious outdoorsperson. Any other low-impact camping skills you learn will be valuable. Being able to keep warm, dry, safe and well fed are essential to a quality experience. It sounds basic but many get in trouble, or at least have a poor experience, because they don't plan properly.

Do-it-yourself rafting trips are popular with those who can't afford a guided float or lodge. These trips allow you to go to Alaska for thousands less than you might spend for top lodges and guides. These trips require extensive planning and preparation, something that is often almost as fun as the trip itself. I hate to get gear-bound but at the same time, having the proper quality equipment is essential.

Your tent should be able to withstand heavy winds and rains, possibly even snow (if you camp into fall) plus have a sealed bug screen. It should be lightweight and freestanding, if possible, to eliminate setup problems in areas where stakes can't be stuck securely into the ground. You may need rocks or logs to sit on the stakes in windy conditions. I've been in enough bad tents to appreciate the difference a good one makes.

Backpacking tents (1-3 person tents) work okay if you need to go ultra-light but lightweight, quality 4- to 8-man (for 2 to 4 persons) expedition tents are better because they are comfortable if it's nasty outside. A heat-generating lantern (gas or candle) will increase the temperature inside enough to help the clothes dry but don't ever leave a lantern, camp stove or gas heater on while you sleep and always vent the tent properly because it may use up the oxygen in the tent and asphyxiate you. Use a ground cloth to save the tent floor. Use a tent that can handle the wind. Four-season tents are best. If you bring a 3-season tent, make sure it has a waterproof bathtub floor, sealed seams, an appropriate rainfly and tie-downs for the wind. Most cheap tents can't handle Alaska's weather and you might find your cheap tent flat in the wind or full of water in the rain.

Your sleeping bag should be good to 20 degrees F. or less. Down bags become useless when wet. Synthetics are a better choice. Keep your sleeping bag in a plastic bag, inside a waterproof dry bag when floating. A good sleeping pad makes a big difference because perfectly level ground is difficult to find. Foam pads should be closed-cell so they don't absorb water. Inflatable pads should be foam filled so they insulate you from the ground. If weight and space are not too critical, take a break-down cot with you for additional comfort. It'll level out a bumpy floor and keep you off damp ground. Make sure the cot legs won't grind holes in the tent floor. For a pillow, just make one using your sleeping bag stuff bag, stuffed full of your next morning's clothing.

In below-freezing temperatures, keep your waders inside the tent and your wading shoes in a sealed, heavy plastic bag, inside your tent. That will hopefully keep them from freezing. Otherwise you'll need to soak them in water before putting them on in the morning.

Your raingear must be high quality. Cheap vinyl units seldom last more than a couple days. Quality waterproof or

69

Kick-boats make great adventure crafts.

breathable/waterproof raingear is a must. If you're extremely lucky, you'll have a week of sunny weather but more often than not you will need to deal with rain and wind. If you can't stay warm and dry you will have a miserable and possibly dangerous trip.

Rafts, rowing frames and oars can be rented from some air-taxi services. Ask about brands and quality. Otherwise, plan on buying or renting a quality raft near home or in Anchorage and air-freighting it up ahead of yourself so that it is there when you arrive. Trying to heft hundreds of pounds of gear through airports isn't much fun and overweight baggage costs can mount but knowing the quality of your gear might be more important. Keep your personal and camping gear lightweight, compact and of moderate or high quality. A rowing frame and oars is preferred because one person can row while others fish. Paddles require most or all to paddle, with little or no float-fishing possible. Modern river kick-boats are a great option to rafts. See the following section for more details.

Sometimes folding kayaks or canoes or inflatable kayaks are desired. They can cover still water in a shorter amount of time but may not handle whitewater rivers very well. Try to avoid large lakes (in a raft) on your float except as a beginning or end because contrary winds may make a real chore out of the crossing.

Few airlines allow camp-stove fuel or stoves on board so you may need to buy or rent it once in Alaska. Planning to cook on fires is an option only if you're good at making fire from wet wood and if you're sure the area has adequate firewood.

Waterproof duffels with backpack straps are very useful. Whatever it takes, keep your sleeping bag and at least one change of clothes dry at all times.

Either buy food at home or in Anchorage. Anchorage has plenty of good shopping stores with packaged foods suitable for river trips. Freeze-dried foods are available in sporting goods stores but are expensive and get pretty bland after a few days. Mix it up with dehydrated or dried foods,

fast water. Try to stick to the main channels when the river braids. Some back channels get clogged with log jams and might require a portage or dragging the raft back upstream. Any Class III or IV whitewater should be scouted and left up to the expert rowers. Portage or line the boat if you have any doubts. Class V water is generally much too risky and should be portaged or avoided altogether. Luckily, most of the best fishing rivers are Class I to III waters.

Class I is flat water to occasional rapids with easy, obstruction-free channels. Class II is frequent rapids with high, regular waves and moderately easy channels, chutes, ledges and drops where the route is easily recognized. Class III is irregular waves in long rapids where back eddies, breakers and rollers require somewhat complex maneuvering and the more difficult chutes, ledges and falls. Class IV is expert only, scouting required, long, very difficult sections of irregular rapids full of powerful back eddies, whirlpools, breakers, sharp bends and constricted canyons. You may want to portage or line the boat through these waters. Class V is lengthy, very difficult rapids with unavoidable haystacks, breakers, rollers, falls, almost impossible chutes where whirlpools and powerful back eddies make the route complicated and dangerous. Scouting is required, as is life insurance, and these sections are almost always portaged. Class VI is nearly impossible even in ideal conditions. Don't even think about it, portage around.

Get a compass and a book on orienteering (map and compass reading). Even better would be investing in a GPS unit. These satellite-linked systems are great for finding your way when used in conjunction with an accurate USGS map that has a GPS grid. GPS units are getting affordable and will tell you where you are with 100 feet or better accuracy. Plot your progress on the map for easy day-by-day planning. Otherwise, you might be guessing at how far you need to go each day to make it to the bottom in time for your pick-up. Maps are available by mail at: USGS Map Sales, 101 12th Ave., #12, Fairbanks, AK 99701.

When on a float trip, make sure on any float trip you bring an appropriate life-vest for each person, wear them! A life-vest won't do you any good strapped to the boat.

Multiple rafts in one group need to stay within eyeshot of each other at all times, especially on large, braided rivers. Getting separated could mean staying separated for the rest of the day or even the trip. This means that each raft be self-sufficient, just in case. A portable CB or marine radio on each raft is of great help in this circumstance. Sattelite phones are valuable for emergencies and are getting cheaper.

Here is a list of suggested equipment for do-it-yourself trips. You will want :

General: Tents, rainfly, ground cloth, stakes, seam sealer, tent repair tape, camp stove, fuel, repair kit, pots, pans,

energy bars, packaged jerky, dried fruits and packaged snack foods. Each serving should be sealed so you don't have open food containers, fresh meat, eggs or fresh fruit for the bears to smell. The best bet is to put food in a bear-resistant container. Take the food packets out of any bulky packaging to save weight and space. See the section on dealing with bears.

You must have a guidebook to floatable rivers in Alaska and a set of detailed maps per boat. The guidebooks are available at Alaska sporting goods stores and bookstores and should include detailed descriptions of each float. Good USGS topographical maps, preferably 7.5 minute quads, are invaluable but realize that river channels can change over time and may vary from your map slightly.

You must also have an experienced rower on each boat. Class I or II rivers are relatively easy to handle and are great places for inexperienced rowers to learn from more experienced rowers. The main dangers are sweepers (trees laying across your path on the river), log jams or sharp rocks in

A happy group begins their backcountry fly-fishing adventure.

dishes, utensils, waterproof matches, waterproof match case, vinyl table cloth (many uses), raft, rowing frame, oars, extra oar, type II, III or V life jackets, raft pump, rope, bailing device, raft repair kit (extra bolts, sewing awl, 5 minute epoxy, wire, duct tape, appropriate patch material, patch glue, cleaning solvent, sandpaper, wrenches, pliers, hack saw, file, small hammer, extra valves), nylon cord, throw bag, compass, topographic maps in clear, watertight case, waterproof gear bags, gear straps, food (# of persons x days x 3 meals + emergency food), food container (preferably bear-resistant), water containers, water filters, small shovel for burying human waste or canister to carry it out if required, rain tarp with guy lines.

Clothing: 2 pair heavy socks, 3 pair light socks (synthetic or wool, no cotton), synthetic or wool pants, swim trunks, t-shirts, shirts, underwear, synthetic thermals, warm coat, sweater, raincoat, rain pants, waterproof boots, camp shoes or sandals, rowing gloves, warm hat, bandana.

Personal: Toothbrush/paste, bathroom tissue, brush/comb, wash cloth, bio soap, insect repellent, first-aid kit, prescription medication, general medication (aspirin, anti-diarrheal, antacid, etc.), sunscreen, ear plugs, duct tape, wallet, emergency phone numbers, credit cards, bank checks, notebook, pencil, water bottle, personal plate, cup, utensils, spices, emergency food bars, snackes, Swiss Army-type knife or Leatherman-style tool, lighter, waterproof matches, candle lantern, waterproof flashlight, batteries, waterproof dry bags for gear, heavy-duty garbage bags, waterproof alarm watch, sleeping bag, sleeping pad.

Fishing: 2 pair polarized fishing glasses, fishing hat, vest or pack, fly boxes, flies, split shot, strike indicators, tapered leaders, tippet spools, hemostats or needle-nose pliers, nippers, fly floatant, fly rods/reels/lines/extra spools, backup fly line, spin rod/reel/line/lures, insect repellent, waders (neoprene or breathable membrane preferred), patch kit, wading shoes, gravel guards, fingerless fishing gloves, rain jacket, whistle or bear bell.

Optional: Camera, film, batteries, water-tight camera case, binoculars, camp lantern, personal stereo, tapes or CDs, extra batteries, reading material, sketchbook, pencils, pens, firearms, ammo, pepper spray, wrist rocket, hiking boots, ski mask, mittens, scarf, mosquito head net, radio, extra folding camp table, folding camp chairs, bag liner, pillow, breakdown cot, razor.

Some of the rainbow trout waters where you might try a do-it-yourself camp or float are the Alagnak River, Alexander Creek, American Creek, Aniak River, Anvik River, Arolik River, Battle Creek, Campbell Creek, Chilikadrotna River, Gibraltar River, Goodnews River, Gulkana River, Kanektok River, Kenai River (upper), Kisaralik River, Koktuli River, Kroto Creek, Kvichak River, Lake Creek, Little Susitna River, Moose Creek, Morraine Creek, Mulchatna River, Naknek River, Newhalen River, Nonvianuk River, Nushagak River, Nuyakuk River, Stuyahok River, Tazimina River, Talachulitna Creek/River, Talkeetna River, Togiak River, Upper Susitna River, Wood River Lakes System. There are many other waters that may not make great floats but would be good fly-ins. Talk to air-taxi companies for their suggestions.

Kick-boating Alaska

The newest and most fun craze in personal adventure craft are the modern kick-boats that are designed for river use. Kick-boats are basically inflatable pontoons connected by a break-down frame and that are small enough to be maneuvered by fins and oars both. This gives the angler his own personal drift boat or lake boat, controlled by fins to leave the arms free to fish. Kick-boats are a blast to float in and many can break down into a package that is easy to check-on, as regular luggage, on airplanes.

I've kick-boated for 14 years from Alaska and Russia to South America. The newest designs are safe enough to recommend them to others. Kick-boats have been getting better since the late 70s but the designs have just gotten up to where they are truly river-worthy for wilderness floats. My kick-boat trips have been full of adventure and fun. They give you a measure of independence that is lacking in raft trips or guided trips. You carry everything you need with you. It's like backpacking on water. You can choose to fish and camp together or separate into small groups in your own lean, mean river machines.

For Alaska, you must have a rocker-hulled, 7 1/2- to 10-foot by 15- to 20-inch diameter pontoon kick-boat with a sturdy frame or frameless design that can break down for transport. It should have a rowing system, foot braces, a cargo area and a tough outer pontoon shell. Currently, Buck's Bags, Dave Scadden Pontoon Craft, J.W Outfitters, Kingfisher, Outcast Sporting Gear, River Otter, Versa-vessel etc. have models that are suitable for the fast rivers in Alaska with light backpacking gear. Check the Internet for more info.

However, don't be fooled by small or poorly designed kick-boats, they can be dangerous. Make sure the company rates them for fast or whitewater river use and that they have a 275- to 500-pound capacity. More importantly, use them on several river trips near home before trying

Alaska. Always float wilderness rivers with at least one other person, and preferably two or three. Never attempt rivers or rapids that are beyond your abilities or the watercraft's rating.

If you choose to go this way, think of the gear you bring in backpacking terms. Keep it lightweight and limit it to the essentials. You'll have to carry everything through airports, check it on as luggage (most airlines have weight restrictions) and get everything, including yourself and your buddies, on a floatplane to and from the water. Excessive gear is counter-productive, but the essentials must be carefully chosen so you don't leave out anything important. Look through the recommended supplies in the previous section and cut that amount down to where you have two large bags (one for the boat—fins, oars, pump and waders—and one for the rest of your personal gear—sleeping bag, tent, etc.). Two bags, 40 to 60 pounds each, plus a carry-on day pack, are plenty for gear, boats, food and shelter for a week if you choose and plan carefully. It's the most adventure for your buck. Check light backpacking Internet sites for ideas.

Fishing Alaska's Road System

There are several good books on fishing Alaska through road access so I won't go into much detail here. Anglers, especially those with young families, may choose to rent a 4-wheel-drive vehicle or motor-home and tour the road system. You may not find the same fishing and wildlife you'll find in fly-out waters, but you should easily find good fishing waters for salmon, trout and steelhead. Char, grayling and northern pike waters are often almost untouched as anglers try the more popular salmon runs. Some rainbow trout lakes and rivers near roads have been supplemented by hatcheries, others are natural.

Read the Alaska fishing and travel guides you find and develop a general itinerary. Play it loose, however, so you can make changes mid-trip if you discover somewhere else you want to try. Ask locals and fishing stores where the fishing is good. Hiring professional fishing guides for a day is a good bet. They will show you the waters and how to fish them. As with any guided trip, ask the guide for specific fishing options.

There are a number of float trips you can do yourself using the road system and your own or a rented watercraft. Hire someone to do a shuttle for you. Some floats are day trips and some require camping along the way. The Upper Kenai River is a good example of a do-it-yourself float trip that has access to large rainbows and salmon, without requiring excessive float-plane fares.

There are many excellent travel and information books on Alaska and it would behoove you to study a few before you plan your trip.

IX

Conclusion

THE CRISP, PUNGENT FOLIAGE SQUEAKS WITH each step of your felt-soled boots. The cool morning air is offset by the quick pace as you and your buddies head for an as yet unseen pristine river. You crest a rise and there it is in the morning fog. A brown bear wading upstream glances over for a second and then lumbers off with a sockeye salmon, to eat in seclusion. You quickly rig as you glance along the river for dark movements in the brush. You tie on your favorite egg pattern and strike indicator as the first shafts of sunlight turn the leaden waters neon. There are several bright-red salmon milling around in the riffle just upstream but you notice a ghostly gray-green shape below them weaving back and forth on the clean gravel.

The cast is made upstream and the line falls nearly silent on the water. It drifts by the giant rainbow without a twitch. Another cast, another untouched drift, could it just be a rainbow colored rock or log? No, it moved again. On the third cast you are beginning to wonder if the big bow wants something else when the indicator shoots across stream and the fish leaps almost before you can set the hook. It rips up the riffle and into the deeper water of the far side of the river bend, jumping madly again before

---

Angler fishes for silver salmon, rainbows, grayling and dollies on remote Alaska river accessed by float plane and kickboats.

taking off downstream. As you begin to chase the fish downstream along the gravel bar you notice your friend has just hooked up as well and his fish shoots upstream under your fly line and jumps right in front of you. He yells, "Fish on" and you grin, saying, "Nice fish" because you know yours is bigger.

The fish begins dogging down and tries to run back up the far side of the run as the reel sings again. Your buddy lands his fish and looks back at you to see why the backing is still showing out the rod tip. He comes to take the obligatory big-fish photo but it's another five minutes before the slab-sided 28-inch native 'bow glides into shallow water and allows the quick Hollywood session. You admire the bright silver side and faint red stripe as you gently revive the fish, then it suddenly powers back into the depths of the run to catch its breath.

You revel in the sense of wilderness, the cold in your fingers, the sun on the hillsides and the satisfying feeling of satiating that primal instinct to interact with nature. There are those who will never understand what it is to really take a walk on the wild side. You're sorry for them. A walk through City Park watching the squirrels and joggers may be as close to nature as many ever get. It's a shame but

you're also glad that they aren't here today, so you can feel true wilderness in the depths of your soul.

Something about the Alaskan experience gets into you and you can't shake it. Maybe it's something that is always in you, seeking an avenue of escape. It motivates you to buck up, take the plunge and never look back, except at the good things, the good friends and the great photos.

If you've never been to Alaska, it's time to start planning. If you have, you'll probably want to return. Whether you want to be wined and dined at a top lodge or you want to float an unknown river by the seat of your pants, Alaska has something for everyone. I go for the fishing but return with much more. To me "Alaska rainbows" is a metaphor for life-enhancing adventure. As varied as the colors of a rainbow in the sky, are the experiences of fishing rainbows in Alaska. Each one is wonderful despite the maelstrom that might accompany the beauty.

I hope you enjoyed this book and that it will help enhance your fishing pleasure. Read it often if it inspires you to new adventures. Alaska will put real meaning into the old cliché "Life doesn't get any better than this." My version would be: "Alaska rainbows put better into life."

Rainbow trout colors.

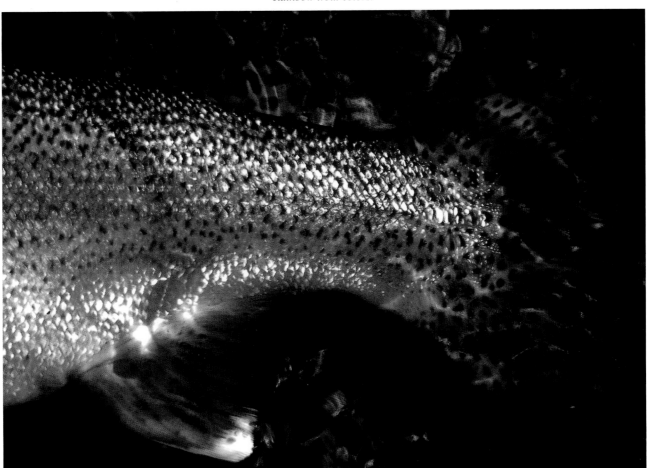

Resources

Books

Alaska Fishing by Rene Limeres & Gunnar Pedersen, Foghorn Press. This is possibly the best all-round reference for anglers deciding where to go, when to go and who to contact. There is more info here than you could ever use, with little fluff.

The *Alaska River Guide* by Karen Jettmar, Alaska Northwest Books, is a great place to get information on various wilderness floats for do-it-yourselfers.

The *Alaska Wilderness Milepost* by Alaska Northwest Books is a good reference for wilderness travelers and adventurers with itsdescriptions of backcountry areas and services.

Alaska Vacation Planner is a free publication from the Alaska Division of Tourism, P.O. Box E, Juneau, AK 99811-0800. Ph. (907) 465-2010.

Flyfishing Alaska by Anthony J. Route, Johnson Books, is a good reference on basic Alaska flyfishing techniques. It will get you into the mindset for whichever species you pursue.

Fly Patterns of Alaska by Alaska Flyfishers Club, Frank Amato Publications, is an interesting collection of Alaska fly patterns with brief descriptions and color photos.

Fly Patterns of Umpqua Feather Merchants by Randall Kaufmann, Umpqua Feather Merchants, is a good fly pattern book that has the tying industry's newest or most popular fly choices with appropriate dressings and great color photos.

The Highway Angler by Gunnar Pedersen is a great reference for the driving angler, whether you drive to Alaska or rent a vehicle once you fly there.

How to Catch Alaska's Trophy Sportfish by Christopher Batin, Alaska Angler Publications, is a good basic reference for all-round fishing in Alaska.

How to Fly Fish Alaska by Jim Repine, Frank Amato Publications, is another good, simple, fishing reference, although slightly outdated.

Safe Travel In Bear Country by Gary Brown, Lyons & Burford Publishers, is a good basic book on black and brown bear habits and how to deal with their presence. (Note: Don't read bear attack books just before your trip.)

Maps

Alaska Atlas & Gazetteer, DeLorme Maps. Topographic maps of the entire state in atlas form. Good for general reference and road systems but not detailed enough for backcountry travel. P.O. Box 298-7000, Freeport, ME 04032. Ph. (800) 227-1656.

Alaska Hunting & Fishing Map, A somewhat useful map with roads, fish locations and records. 5140 E. 104th Ave., Anchorage, AK 99516. Ph. (907) 346-2193.

The Maps Place, Great source for any Alaska USGS and NOAA nautical and aeronautical maps. 3545 Arctic Blvd., Anchorage, AK 99503. Ph. (907) 562-6277.

U.S. Geological Survey, The main distribution center of USGS maps. Box 25286, Federal Center, Denver, CO 80225.

Alaska Rainbow Trout Lodges & Outfitters

These are a few of the lodges that have good reputations for getting fly anglers into rainbows and salmon. There are others, and owners can change, so look at who is advertising in your fishing magazines and write for literature and references.

Alaska's Rainbow Adventures, Quality float trips for rainbows and other Alaska species. Contact: Paul Hansen, P.O. Box 456, Anchor Point, AK 99556. Ph. (907) 235-2647.

Alaska's Wilderness Lodge, Float-planes and jet boats to quality waters. P.O. Box 190748, Anchorage, AK 99519. Ph. (800) 835-8032.

Alaska Wilderness Expeditions, Outfitted river float-trips for various species. Tim White. Ph. (888) 494-5325. E-mail: akfishguide@chastnet.com.

Alaska Wildwater, Statewide equipment rentals, including tents, rafts and kayaks. P.O. Box 110615, Anchorage, AK 99511.

Bristol Bay Anglers, Focuses on the trophy trout of the Naknek River and has fly-outs available to Brooks River, etc. Chip Henward (Nov.-May) 5225 Paradise Canyon Road, Paradise Valley, AZ 85253, Ph. (602) 951-8946, Fax (602) 991-5939. (June-October) P.O. Box 355, King Salmon, Alaska 99613, Ph. (907) 246-3660.

Bristol Bay Lodge, Well-established lodge with fly-outs and out-camps. Ron McMillan, 2422 Hunter Rd., Ellensburg, WA 98926, Ph. (509) 964-2094.

Crystal Creek Lodge, An established Orvis-endorsed lodge with jet boat, float-plane and helicopter transportation. Dan Michaels, P.O. Box 92170, Anchorage, AK 99509-2170, Ph. (800) 525-3153. E-mail: crystalc@alaska.net. Net: http://www.crystalcreeklodge.com.

Dave Duncan & Sons, Alaskan Outfitter, A selection of fresh- and saltwater trips, float-trips and base-camp trips are available. High Valley Ranch, 4630 Weaver Rd., Ellensburg, WA 98926. Ph. (509) 962-1060.

Iliaska Lodge, A quality lodge with jet boat and fly-out fishing. Ted Gerken, (May 1-Oct. 1) P.O. Box 228, Iliamna AK 99606, Ph. (907) 571-1221. (Oct. 1-May 1) 6160 Farpoint Dr., Anchorage, AK 99507, Ph. (907) 337-9844. Net: www.alaska.net/~Iliaska.

Katmai Lodge, A large, established lodge on the Alagnak River that can accommodate 40-plus anglers at a time. Jet-boating to good spots and fly-outs are available. Fishing in Kamchatka, Russia also. Tony Sarp, 2825 90th St., SE, Everett, WA 98208. Ph. (206) 337-0326, Fax: (206) 337-0335, E-mail: <alaska@katmai.com. Net: www.katmai.com.

Ouzel Expeditions, Ecology-minded fishing and sightseeing expeditions in Alaska and Russia. P.O. Box 935, Girdwood AK 99587. Ph. (800) 825-8196.

Rainbow King Lodge, Comfortable lodge with jet-boat and fly-out trips. Ph. 1-800-458-6539.

Rainbow Point Lodge, Nice lodge with many rainbow trout waters nearby. 1441 S. Pennsylvania #02, Casper, WY 82609. Ph. 1-877-850-5858 or 1-617-899-2326.

Rainbow River Lodge, One of the premier lodges that caters to rainbow trout anglers. Jet-boat on the famous Copper River and fly-outs for various species of game fish. Chris Goll, 4127 Raspberry Rd., Anchorage, AK 99502. Ph. (907) 243-7894.

Air-Taxi Operators

Branch River Air Service, For backcountry flights to Bristol Bay waters, originating at the town of King Salmon. 4540 Edinburgh Dr., Anchorage AK 99516. Ph. (907) 248-3539 in winter, in summer call (907) 246-3437

Freshwater Adventures, For backcountry flights and trips originating from Dillingham. P.O. Box 62, Dillingham, AK 99576. Ph. (907) 243-7676 in winter, in summer call (907) 842-5060.

Jay Hawk Air, Flights for sightseeing, unguided fishing & hunting trips. 1842 Merrill Field Dr., Anchorage, AK 99509. Ph. (907) 276-4404.

Ketchum Air Service, Flights to fishing cabins, float trips, lodges and scenic areas. N. Shore Lake Hood, Anchorage, AK 99509. Ph. (907) 243-5525.

Iliamna Air Taxi, Backcountry flights to and from some of the best rainbow trout waters around Lake Iliamna. P.O. Box 109, Iliamna AK 99606. Ph. (907) 571-1248.

Peninsula Airways, For flights to locations on the Alaskan Peninsula. 4851 Aircraft Dr., Anchorage AK 99502. Ph. (907) 243-2485 or (800)448-4226.

Tikchik Airventures, Float plane shuttles and raft rentals for do-it-yourselfers. P.O. Box 71, Dillingham, AK 99576. Ph. (907) 842-5841.

Statewide Resources

Alaska Department Of Fish & Game, Write for a copy of current regulations. P.O. Box 25526, Juneau, AK 99802-5526. Ph. (907) 465-4112. Fax: (907) 465-3088.

Alaska Public Lands Information Center, Information on state and national parks, refuges and forests. 605 W. Fourth Ave., Suite 105, Anchorage, AK 99501-5162. Ph. (907) 271-2737.

U.S. Forest Service Information Center-For info on Alaska's National Forests (fishing and rental cabins). Centennial Hall, 101 Egan Dr., Juneau, AK 99801. Ph. (907) 586-8751.

Bureau Of Land Management, Information on non-designated federal lands, rental cabins and the Wild and Scenic Rivers. 222 W. Seventh Ave., Suite 13, Anchorage, AK 99513. (907) 271-5960.

Note: There are many other resources on the internet now. Just do a search on the subjects or places in which you are interested.

Index

FLY PATTERNS OF ALASKA
Alaska Flyfishers (Revised and enlarged edition)

Definitive fly pattern book containing the best 251 patterns for fly fishing for most species of game fish in Alaska. These flies were carefully selected by an editorial team led by Dirk V. Dirksen of the Alaska Flyfishers and were magnificently photographed in color by club member Michael Scarbrough. We have printed them on top-quality, thick, glossy paper in large format size and with sewn binding for ease when tying. Pattern description, originator (when known) and fishing history of each fly is included. In addition there are many outstanding scenic Alaska photographs depicting the glories of Alaska and its fishing. This is an outstanding fly tying, coffee table book that you will not want to put down for its beauty and utility! 8 1/2 x 11, 80 pages.
SB: $19.95   **ISBN: 1-878175-31-9**

NYMPH FISHING
Dave Hughes

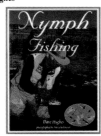

This masterful all-color, large-format book by one of America's favorite angling writers will teach you what you need to know to fish nymphs effectively, with crisp text and dramatic color photos by Jim Schollmeyer. Color plates and dressings of author's favorite nymphs. All the techniques and methods learned here will guarantee that on the stream or lake your nymph imitation will be fishing right! 8 1/2 x 11 inches, 56 pages.
SB: $19.95   **ISBN: 1-57188-002-X**

COLOR GUIDE TO STEELHEAD DRIFT FISHING
Bill Herzog

Each year nearly 1,000,000 steelhead are hooked in North America and the great majority of these fish are hooked using drift fishing techniques. This lavishly illustrated, all-color guide is the "bible" if you want to get in on the action. Written by one of America's greatest drift fishermen, you will learn the techniques that can guarantee your entry into the 10% of the anglers who hook 90% of the steelhead. This is a heavy-duty graduate course! 8 1/2 x 11 inches, 80 pages.
SB: $16.95   **ISBN: 1-878175-59-9**

SPINNER FISHING FOR STEELHEAD, SALMON & TROUT
Jed Davis

The "bible" for spinner fishing and the most in-depth, non-fly-fishing book ever written about steelhead and their habits. Information on how to make spinners is complete, including how to assemble, obtain parts, even how to silver plate. The fishing techniques, lure, line color and size selection, and reading fish-holding water sections are excellent. 8 1/2 x 11 inches, 97 pages.

SB: $19.95   **ISBN: 0-936608-40-4**

ALASKA FISHING ON A BUDGET
Bernard R. Rosenberg

Have you always wanted to go fishing in Alaska, but figured it was way out of your budget? If so, then this book is for you. Bernard has almost 20 years of experience planning spin fishing trips to Alaska at a very affordable price. This complete trip-planning book includes: resources; timing your trip; best fishing locations; arranging your flight and itinerary; vehicle rental; equipment and necessities to bring; protection from bugs, bears, and rain; packing for the trip; stocking up in Anchorage; on the road; techniques; preserving and processing your catch; etiquette; and so much more. Bernard can orchestrate the perfect trip for the minimum amount of money, follow his blueprint and you can't go wrong. 6 x 9 inches, 111 pages.
SB: $14.95   **ISBN: 1-57188-297-9**

DRIFT BOAT FLY FISHING
A River Guide's Sage Advice
Neale Streeks

Streeks is a professional trout guide in Montana. Over the years he has amassed a very impressive amount of practical and "inside" fly fishing information that is presented in his all-color book. It is extremely helpful for the wading angler, too. This is a meaty book that, if followed, will make you one of the very best fly anglers on the stream! Hatches, flies, tactics, water reading, equipment, etc. A masterpiece of information. 8 1/2 x 11 inches, 112 pages.
SB: $29.95   **ISBN: 1-57188-016-X**

DRIFTBOATS
A Complete guide
Dan Alsup

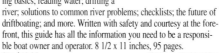

Driftboats have a long, and at times controversial, history in their native Oregon. Commonplace on Pacific Northwest waters, the popularity of driftboats is enjoying a surge eastward and today are found in every state. Now comes a comprehensive guide to driftboats, this book covers: the history; the controversy; contemporary boats; purchasing and outfitting a driftboat; rowing basics; reading water; drifting a river; solutions to common river problems; checklists; the future of driftboating; and more. Written with safety and courtesy at the forefront, this guide has all the information you need to be a responsible boat owner and operator. 8 1/2 x 11 inches, 95 pages.
SB: $19.95   **ISBN: 1-57188-189-1**

SPOON FISHING FOR STEELHEAD
Bill Herzog

One of the most effective ways to hook steelhead (as well as salmon) is with a spoon. Bill Herzog covers spoon fishing techniques for the full year, going into finishes, sizes, weights, shapes, water temperature differences, winter and summer fish differences, commercial and custom spoons, spoon parts suppliers, and reading water. Scores of color photos printed on thick, glossy, quality paper enhance the learning experience along with many line drawings, graphs and illustrations. If you like to fish for steelhead and salmon you will find the information in this book to be invaluable—regardless of how you fish. This is a very revealing, post-graduate fishing technique book sure to please! 8 1/2 x 11 inches, 64 pages.
SB: $14.95   **ISBN: 1-878175-30-0**

FLOATING ALASKA!
Planning Self-Guided Fishing Expeditions
Don Crane

Alaska is a dream destination for many fishermen, but with this book those dreams can now come true. Don Crane takes a complicated topic and breaks it down so that anyone can plan a self-guided float trip for an extremely reasonable price. Crane covers: preparation; gear; camping; food; fishing; wildlife; resources and services; and so much more. If you and your buddies have always fantasized about an Alaskan fishing adventure, *Floating Alaska!* will tell you everything you need to know for a productive, inexpensive, and organized trip. 6 x 9 inches, 80 pages.
SB: $15.95   **ISBN: 1-57188-338-X**

ADVANCED FLY FISHING FOR STEELHEAD
Deke Meyer

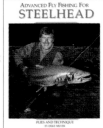

All-color book explains the most effective fly-fishing techniques for steelhead and the best contemporary flies to use. Chapters on: fly design; Spey flies; wet-flies; dry-flies; small-stream fishing; shooting heads; winter steelheading; two-handed rods; nymphing; deep drifting flies; and much more. Gorgeous book full of fly tying help and material preparation suggestions. Grand color plates of finest producing flies including pattern descriptions. With technique information and fly patterns presented you should be able to successfully fly fish for steelhead anywhere throughout the year. 8 1/2 x 11 inches, 160 pages, all color.
SB: $29.95   **ISBN: 1-878175-10-6**

FLIES: THE BEST ONE THOUSAND
Randle Scott Stetzer

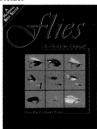

Incredibly beautiful all-color pattern and dressing guide of best flies for trout, salmon, steelhead, bass, and saltwater species. Most shown actual size or larger. Marvel at the tiers and photographer's art as you use it over and over researching flies to tie or when preparing for a trip. Stetzer is an expert fly tier as well as guide. 8 1/2 x 11 inches, 128 pages.

SB: $24.95   **ISBN: 1-878175-20-3**

FLIES OF THE NORTHWEST
Inland Empire Fly Fishing Club

A fully revised, all-color edition of the most popular fly pattern book for the Northwest, including Western Canada, by the Inland Empire Fly Fishing Club of Spokane, Washington. The best 200 flies for trout, steelhead, and salmon. Each fly, individually photographed by Jim Schollmeyer, includes dressing, originator, and how to fish and tie it. Color paintings throughout. Full-color, 6 by 9 inches, 136 pages.
SPIRAL SB: $24.95   **ISBN: 1-57188-065-8**